THIS BOOK IS DEDICATED
TO ALL READERS
AND ALL THOSE WHO SEEK ANSWERS

May you be blessed with

intense curiosity,
deep compassion,
the desire to overcome all obstacles,
and the thirst to fully understand

for these will move you forward on your spiritual path,
enabling you to contribute to the
rebuilding of a new world

My deepest gratitude goes to Seraphin
for his trust and for the wisdom he has provided

Thank you to all translators, proof-readers and video makers
for their dedication to the Seraphin material

Rosie Jackson

There are other words which you do not use often. We can make a list: divine, holy, sacred, mission, vocation, cosmos, celestial, consecrated, infinity and eternity. Yet all these words, and the understanding of what they really mean, and the areas to which they apply, and the "power and the glory" which they entail, are so far from your thinking processes, whereas they are intended to be AT YOUR VERY CORE

Seraphin offers us not only a larger perspective but a very positive one: he assures us that – whatever might seem to be happening to the contrary – we are in divine hands. It is not the destiny of this planet to self-destruct, although this is the path which the majority of its inhabitants are collectively pursuing.

Celestials who are closely observing our planet have stepped in many times to prevent such self-destruction, notably after World War Two when earth was in danger of doing a pole flip. They are waiting for the right moment to take on a more visible role, to provide us with more concrete guidance and to encourage us to make all our decisions in favour of humanity and of earth, our benefactress.

In view of all the present conflict and suffering, "waiting" for celestial intervention may seem torturous. However, surrender to divine timing and to our own divine role is paramount, and this volume contains three very poignant messages on the subject of surrender. Seraphin defines surrender as "recognising ultimate wisdom and aligning oneself with that wisdom, in order to better serve humanity".

It may seem like there is no end to the present disturbing developments. There is no doubt, however, that an "end" will finally arrive, just as there is no doubt that a house built on lies is bound to fall, and just as there is no doubt that a balloon which is continuously filled with hot air is bound to burst.

The end marks the start of a chaotic, traumatic but ultimately glorious new beginning. Seraphin continuously assures us that "the light of day inevitably follows the dark night".

This 6th volume of THE COMPLETE SERAPHIN MESSAGES consists of three parts.

The first is a compilation of the most recent Seraphin Messages.

The second is entitled THE PIONEER EXERCISE MANUAL. Everyone remaining on earth will be guided to overcome trauma and develop a pioneering spirit. These exercises further such growth.

The third part contains many constructive texts which start with the sentence THE WORLD WILL BECOME PEACEFUL, BEAUTIFUL AND ABUNDANT IF. This is a continuation of my previous book of that name.

All these texts have been written during the last two years under the guidance of Seraphin, to whom my eternal gratitude.

This introduction ends with two previous messages called:

THE PURPOSE OF THESE MESSAGES and
THOUGH I WALK THROUGH THE VALLEY OF DEATH

This is because they are so relevant to our present global predicament.

May you travel well through the valley of death and may you be commended for continuing your journey and contributing to the flourishing of a new era.

With gratitude, Rosie Jackson

Seraphin Message 260:
THE PURPOSE OF THESE MESSAGES:

1. PREPARATION FOR MAGNETIC REVERSAL
   AND EVACUATION

2. A MANUAL FOR SPIRITUAL LIVING

3. A DEMONSTRATION OF CELESTIAL CONTACT

Some of you may ask why this scribe has been receiving my thoughts and posting my messages over the last few years. This is not a fanciful preoccupation, undertaken during leisure time. This is an essential introduction to new courses of behaviour and instructions on how to improve your perceptions of yourselves and your interactions.

This is – and I will repeat this – ESSENTIAL DUE TO THE VERY DEPLORABLE STATE OF AFFAIRS ON YOUR PLANET, ALL OF WHICH HAVE RESULTED FROM NEGLIGENT BEHAV-IOUR. It is not that we are harping on, pointing fingers and criti-cising. It is that we are attempting to PREVENT THE GLOBAL BOAT FROM CAPSIZING.

And we say again: these messages are not PREVENTIVE MEASURES OR POLITE SUGGESTIONS WHICH YOU MIGHT READ ON SUNDAYS. THEY ARE POINTING YOU TOWARDS THE ONLY DIRECTION WHICH WILL SAVE YOU FROM SELF DESTRUCTION. THE ANSWER TO ALL OF YOUR SORROWS IS THE SPIRITUAL REVOLUTION IN YOURSELVES, hence the name of the project initiated with our scribe – a project which en-courages understanding across all nations, all religions and all social circumstances.

Why do we send out these messages?

BECAUSE THE SITUATION IS CRITICAL.

Your earth is burdened to a degree of no return.
Yet she will return, and so will you if you enter fully into the change of heart we have been suggesting.

Our purpose is to encourage you to always make decisions IN EARTH'S FAVOUR, even in (and especially in) the smallest of issues, which are in reality very important issues if seen from a cumulative aspect where billions of people are involved, for she has been your benevolent benefactress for many many thousands of years. To ignore this is encouraging your peril.

Why do we send out this message?

BECAUSE THE TIME OF FINAL CHOOSING IS READILY APPROACHING, AND BECAUSE THE EARTH HAS CHOSEN TO REJECT ALL NEGATIVITY LOADED UPON HER.

This she will do by moving and shaking. This she will do by slowing down the pace of her rotation and stopping. This is what you call a "magnetic reversal".

Before she comes to a standstill, and before the major disruptions of earth and water which accompany this scenario actually occur, you as the global population will be given the chance to be lifted off out of danger, if necessary.

This operation will be conducted by friendly galactic forces operating for your sole benefit. These messages are therefore an education program leading to this point. The main emphasis and learning scenario at the present time is LETTING GO. Your world is about to change, and the most critical question is: CAN YOU CHANGE WITH IT?

The secondary purpose of these messages is to demonstrate that communication with off-planet beings (so-called "angels", of which there are myriad varieties) is possible, and that this is in fact a great benefit for personal development and – if well received and circulated – a great benefit for global development.

So, we warn you again: this has all been preparation for your coming decision:

Will you accept celestial help coming to you, or not?

Will you seriously contemplate the dangers perpetrated by your behaviours of not?

Whether on earth before or after the reversal, you can be sure that YOUR BEHAVIOUR COUNTS – that it is in fact essential for the rebuilding of the sick society into which you have collectively degenerated.

THE EARTH WILL ROTATE SLOWER AND EVENTUALLY STAND STILL. THEN IT WILL BE YOUR MOVE.

Then it will be your choice whether to evacuate *(NB: this will only happen in extreme circumstances)*, thus managing to leave everything behind, or to choose to remain and perish. These are the alternatives. There is no middle way.

We thank this scribe, for she does not like to put out such strong words, yet they are necessary at this time.

DON'T SHOOT THE MESSENGER FOR THIS MESSAGE.

Instead, look around you – at the violence, the lack of compassion, the deliberate destruction, the lack of beauty, the debased morals, the pollution, and ask yourselves

HOW CAN THIS BE?

Not until you have investigated and discovered the very root of this within yourselves will you also rediscover the divine purpose in yourselves which is to restore this earth to her former glory through your optimal behaviour.

This period of renewal will follow your stay in the spaceships (even now, waiting for you) when you return to an earth freed of dark forces, spinning in a new direction.

(NB: evacuation takes place in the case of a pole flip, which is the worst-case scenario and which is not presently on the cards. Evacuation could take place in areas afflicted by danger)

Yes, this is a chaotic and tumultuous phase, and there is no way of avoiding these consequences of humanity's behaviour. The law of cause and effect has caught up with you. To change this situation is the purpose of our frequent messages, and to turn you towards a life which is blessed through your intrinsic knowledge of your ability to create paradise in alignment with the sacred laws. All this shall you learn, should you choose to continue with earth for this purpose.

So you see: all this, as all else, pivots on YOUR CHOICE.

Your choice now is whether to spread this message (and previous ones) far and wide, or not. Your choice is to take over responsibility, to assist those who feel helpless and stranded, to calm those afflicted by fear, and to help everyone board the ships when they arrive. There will be no overlooking this.

We ask you to be in readiness and we thank you for your attention throughout this message.

Seraphin

Seraphin Message 348:

THOUGH I WALK THROUGH THE VALLEY OF DEATH; FEARS AND FACTS

Imagine you can see two tall mountains in the hazy distance. If you look out of the window of your vehicle in that particular direction, you may see them, and you may see them approach ever closer. Yet if your hands are on the steering wheel constantly, and if you are concentrating on getting through heavy traffic, you will not take in the full height and magnificence of these mountains. Instead you may be swerving, cruising or stopping for some distraction along the way.

But the journey WILL continue and you WILL move ever nearer to them. Their outlines become ever clearer and ever darker until you find yourself directly between them and completely in their shadow, from one moment to the next. At this point the words THOUGH I WALK THROUGH THE VALLEY OF DEATH may occur to you, for the daylight is lost, your car lights fail to work and there is no way of orientating yourself. An icy wind begins to blow. You know that if you stay in your car, you will probably not survive, so you override your fear, get out and start to GIVE VOICE, hoping that someone else will answer with a supporting word, hoping that someone else will light a match, hoping that the great swathe of uneasiness will dissipate. You must GIVE VOICE, or you will be cut by the wind, lashed by the rain, left to "wild animals" and presumed dead.

Many will automatically scream OH GOD, and indeed talking to "God", which is in essence talking to the divine part of yourself as a fractal of the GREAT CREATION, is the optimal path, and trust in this path means losing your FEAR. This is the juncture at which you find yourselves, Beloveds. Will you panic in fear or will you find that incorruptible sacred part of yourself and use this base to connect with others, consolidating facts and telling your own personal stories? Will you "lighten" the burdens you carry and thus doing so compassionately lighten the burdens of others which have been carried through millennia of "darkness"? Will you "seize the day" at that very moment of being stranded and alone, or will you succumb to the darkness and to the predators who created it?

We suffer for you as we see you approach this "gnashing of teeth" which is the inevitable outcome for some – for those who decide never to admit and never to relent, who thrash around wildly with their cries of war, flailing around dangerously and defiantly in the dark, eternally proud of the contribution they made towards its creation and continued maintenance. With those who step out bravely and tell all, who gather audiences, who stalwartly exhume their most painful experiences in order to enlighten others, we pledge our protection and support. We wrap you in our arms and commend you for deciding that the fate of humanity is more important than the fate of yourself, for you are those who blow the whistle so that others can avoid danger and see so clearly that they can take concrete and decisive action to ensure that such episodes never again ensue. Seraphin

Seraphin Message 451:
THE TAPESTRY OF TRANSFORMATION

Through Rosie, 21st June 2021

Today is the summer solstice, Beloveds, and as usual there are those among you who are all hyped up, proclaiming spectacular changes and transformations to happen on this very specific date. How many times will you succumb to this? How many times will you be taken in, rather than using every second to further a positive agenda YOURSELVES and to reverse the dreadful situation you have on your hands WITH YOUR OWN HANDS AND THROUGH YOUR OWN EFFORT? We urge you, as ever, to move swiftly into your own sovereignty and to stalwartly support all those around you who allow you to do so.

We are going to talk about transformation today, which has nothing to do with magically transforming or transitioning into a new form or a new world or a new situation without personal effort. It does not happen in a moment.

It CAN happen in a moment, but this does not depend on an outer catalyst (though this may help, and though this is in the pipeline): it depends on your RECEPTIVITY to new impulses and your own DECISION to behave differently AFTER RECEIVING the new impulses or information. Rather than being a sudden change, transformation is a CONTINUOUS PROCESS,.

Transformation, if it is to be lasting and "complete" (though nothing is ever complete due to constant evolving), must involve dedication on a continuous basis. It is not one large decision or one momentous change in behaviour: it is continually adhering to HIGH MORAL PRINCIPLES AND WORTHY GOALS. It is not a sudden "sweeping away" of all evil elements (though this is also in the pipeline, arranged by your galactic brethren who hold you dearly in their hearts) but through concentrated and co-operative effort to PREVENT ANY BUDS OF EVIL BLOOMING AGAIN.

Transformation is not throwing a ball into a pond and making a big splash. It is not climbing a mountain and screaming EUREKA. It is not making an impassioned speech before thousands of people. It is a daily practice, where each thought and each action is a strand of delicate thread, chosen for exactly that moment and that time, to be woven with care, together with all other strands offered by other earth inhabitants, who have similarly chosen exactly that thread and that time to insert their input into the common TAPESTRY.

We are using this image to again stress the importance of your every move, and to remind you of your critical role in extremely difficult times, soon to become much more difficult.

What is the tapestry you are co-creating? What picture or vision will it show? Will it last well, due to the quality of the material and the skill of craftsmanship, or will it quickly show "wear and tear" due to inappropriate material, shoddy work and time "taken off".

We know that our tone has been, and still is, very stern. This is because your situation is so serious. It will require great determination to build something which is durable and closely woven. It will require a JOINT VISION, even before you start, otherwise you will not be able to co-ordinate the weaving process. It means that you have to jointly decide on the direction, the process, the colours and the thickness of yarn PREVIOUS TO STARTING.

You can view the already existing threads (on which the tapestry will be woven) as the cosmic laws, to which you are required to adhere. They set the scene. They provide the framework. They determine the direction and hold the whole structure of the tapestry in place. And when you have finished weaving, it is those threads which will be cut off and knotted and which will hold the whole tapestry firmly in place. If even one of those threads is cut, frayed or overstretched (meaning if cosmic law is disregarded or if observance of same are lax) then the tapestry will develop a hole or a boil, and the picture or vision will suffer.

What part will you play in all this, Beloveds? Have you got the stamina to hold out until the end of this confusing period, to let go of all and to start a new period in earth's history in the way we have just described? Think well on this, for it is a decision which will be required of you all. We are waiting in the wings. Seraphin.

Seraphin Message 452:
THE DIVINE BACKDROP AND HOLY WORK

Through Rosie, 29th June 2021

Perhaps you are wondering, Beloveds on Earth, what we mean by "the divine backdrop". What is divine, in your eyes, and is it in in the forefront, or in the background, or is it in your range of vison at all?

Maybe "divine" is not a word you use often. Maybe divinity is not something you contemplate often in the course of your busy, mundane lives which centre very much on the material and the superficial. There are other words which you do not use often. We can make a list: divine, holy, sacred, mission, vocation, cosmos, celestial, consecrated, infinity and eternity. Yet all these words, and the understanding of what they really mean, and the areas to which they apply, and the "power and the glory" which they entail, are so far from your thinking processes, whereas they are intended to be AT YOUR VERY CORE.

If they are at the CENTRE of your actions, and if they compass your every step, your every mode of behaviour and your every decision, your lives will transform rapidly into purposeful, fulfilling and exhilarating adventures. Is it not this that you imagine for yourselves, citizens of earth?

That your constricted, humdrum lives expand beyond measure, that you live your HOLY POTENTIAL
and that you create SACRED SPACES
and create a GLORIOUS FUTURE which stretches out
FOR ALL ETERNITY ACROSS THE COSMOS?

It is our intention to stretch your minds, to move them away from hopping here and there from one event to the next, from one video to the next, from one piece of information to the next, from one day to the next, from one meal to the next, and from one useless and insignificant pastime to the next.

WE ASK YOU TO OPEN YOUR ARMS
AND RECEIVE EVERYTHING THAT WE, YOUR GUIDES,
ARE PREPARED TO GIVE YOU.
THIS IS ACTUALLY
THE WORLD, AND THE COSMOS, AND ETERNITY.

We would surely love to rip you out of your present circumstances and show you the stars, the endless horizons, the countless variations of life on other planets, the joy of interacting and finding common denominators with those who are so different to your selves but who will UPLIFT YOU FAR BEYOND THAT WHICH YOU HAVE HITHERTO EXPERIENCED.

Yet, we require your permission. We require your trust. We require your unconditional love for everything and everyone that comes your way. We require you to develop a mission. We require you to be completely open to what we show you. We require to you to act when you encounter something which does not fulfil the criteria of the DIVINE. We require you to react immediately if anything is out of alignment with cosmic law.

Can you fulfil these, criteria, Beloveds? Is your behaviour commendable, in every area of your actions, every day anew? Know that your OPPORTUNITIES to act in this enlightened way will increase exponentially as we enter the final and very acute stages of this planetary transition.

This transition is RELATED TO YOURSELVES. It is not simply something which happens, and to which you will (or will not) adapt. It is part of your every breath, and your every breath will either encourage its pace, or will drag the whole process out even longer.

So, tread carefully, Beloveds, knowing the incredible power of your footprint, and the incredible range of influence which your words have. Your words and thoughts travel universes. Your acts of courage and kindness can inspire a million onlookers. Your unconditional love can travel to far flung galaxies from one second to the next.

We have often referred to the "unseen worlds", as we do today, to inspire you to continue walking the road "less travelled". It is again our intention to inspire you with your own possibilities in these times of great change and distress.

May you always be aware of the DIVINE BACKDROP,
which oversees all situations, and may you always complete
HOLY WORKS, so that you blend in with this divine backdrop.

Thus will you merge as one.

Thus will the present divine backdrop cease to remain in the background. It will come to the foreground and envelop all.

Seraphin

Seraphin Message 453: THE GREAT BELL TOLLS

Through Rosie, 10th July 2021

The great bell tolls, Beloved Citizens of Earth, whether you hear it or not, whether you "believe in it" or not, whether you are set against it or not, and whether you are indifferent to it or not, you will be affected.

We have given previous messages concerning a bell ringing, and in these cases, we were referring to the bell which rings at the end of a lesson (and we hope that the lesson has been learnt. The education, at least, has been provided by so many masters and adepts). Maybe you heard their voices, maybe you did not, but they have been visiting your earth plane for many generations, in the hope of helping you rise from your self-created misery, by helping you realise the godliness of YOURSELVES and of your DIVINE ACTS, if in synchronicity with DIVINE WILL. For this, you should be grateful. For their "sacrifice" and for their determination, you should be on your knees in gratitude, yet for the great majority, this has remained unseen and unheard. This is why, now, the small bells have no more use. It requires an enormous bell to wake you up.

Some of you may be aware of the power of sound, and that it has a strong vibration. This bell will sound so loudly that its vibration will carry along the circumference of the earth (and yes, it is round, for those who are sunken in scepticism to the degree that they think it could be flat), until it returns to its place of origin.

As it passes, this vibration will be affected by everything it passes through, collecting information on the way. It is a method of sieving out information, and also a way to encourage cleansing. No one will be spared this experience, for sound and vibration travel endlessly, and they pervade all. They purge whatever lies in their path. They are like fire, consuming dross and preparing the ground for future growth.

Whether you see the symbolism in these words or not is an indicator of your own level of spiritual growth. This sound will leave some people cold. They will never generate the heat or the energy to move into a different level of action, or to generate the next level of compassion, which is all-encompassing.

With other people, every cell will "heat up", as in energized, and thus they will – as a result of their own flexible mind-set – rise in potential and in spiritual growth in that new insights will not only be received but also integrated immediately so that there is no "backlog" to be processed.

In the end, these are the ones who will never experience trauma again, even if they are placed in the midst of dreadful circumstances, because they have processed all previous trauma immediately. They will actually welcome all challenges, knowing that they can be overcome. They will not hesitate. They will flow like rivers into every crevice, searching for every possibility, uncovering every stone and every difficulty, sweeping all rubbish ahead of them in a raging torrent, clearing all the banks of superfluous and flimsy constructions, and thus acting as purging agents themselves, in the same way that this "great bell" will soon sweep through your lands.

Everyone will experience this differently, according to their own constitution and development, yet we hope, through this imagery, to have helped you to imagine what is to come.

Seraphin

Seraphin Message 454:
INTERRUPTIONS AND BURNING BRIDGES

Through Rosie, 22nd July 2021

Dearly beloved inhabitants of earth: we survey how events are unfolding in your lives, and we see that the "normal" flow of things is stopped by two phenomena – interruptions and burning bridges.

The interruptions may start as small distractions which are not capable of making you change direction, or which stop your course of action only temporarily, yet these will increase in power and number, in the same way that many small rivulets will join at some stage to become a mighty river. The force of this will make you "move" in a new direction, whether you want to or not. The power of such rivers, especially if exacerbated or if attempts have been made to keep them under control with dams or similar measures, is extremely great, as can be seen in the many floods you are experiencing worldwide at the moment.

Such natural "disasters" are on the increase, yet they are not disasters in the sense of unavoidable tragedies: they are part of a cleansing process which is necessary because of the pain and irregularities and exploitation which YOU have carried out on earth's crust.

The EFFECTS of all these have cumulated,
and earth sees no other way out than to
RESIST FURTHER MALTREATMENT and to
CLEANSE HERSELF.

Interruptions are difficult to bear for some. Yet they awaken you earth citizens to what is important and what is of real value. Loss of material goods, for example, as opposed to loss of moral principles, is nothing in the long run. To possess nothing, from one moment to the next, can be a great moment of change from which you – naked in all senses of the word – can restart your lives without unnecessary baggage. Whether you spend the next 20 or 30 years lamenting your loss, or whether you pull yourselves together and launch with enthusiasm on a new path, is completely up to you. This may sound hard, but you are sovereign beings who decide on your next course of action.

We remind you also that
such events are beneficial in that they are
INTERRUPTING YOUR INSANITY
and they provide a stage on which you can
RELEARN A NEW WAY OF LIVING IN MUTUAL HARMONY.

As with any situations at the present time, the opposite is true. And tragic interruptions of all kinds actually serve to usher in paradise. This may be an outrageous statement for your ears, yet long term, it is the absolute truth.

The second phenomenon you are observing is BURNING BRIDGES. Water, as we have just mentioned, is an element of cleansing, and fire is also in this category. Even on very basic levels, "fire" is a purifying force. If you have a headache, it is because you are harbouring a suppressed BURNING QUESTION which is being ignored but which wants to "burn" its way into the open, into your consciousness. If something is ignored, it will burn all the more brightly, or become all the more explosive during your negligence or refusal to open your eyes.

You will see more and more inflammatory speeches, examples of burning anger, cases of burning enthusiasm, and widespread destruction by fire. Fire is something which can rarely be contained, like a large river which bursts its banks. And all these phenomena are related to the disposition of the earth who has lost her temper with you (who are her destroyers) and this is equivalent to strong emotions which translate in reality into heat, fire and a gathering of destructive events and intensity.

In this scenario, you cannot separate the feelings and wishes of your mother earth from yourselves. You are inextricably entwined. You have subjected her to excesses. For millennia she has chosen, despite this negativity, to nurture and protect you. She has been an all-indulgent mother, trying to help her progeny. Yet she has received scant attention in return, and now her instinct of self-survival rises above all else. She is the future breeding ground for a higher level of soul. This means that humans of a high spiritual level will be acceptable to her as citizens. Those who act selfishly will not be accepted by her. She has given her citizens / children a lot of leeway, so that they might learn, but there comes a time in all mother / child relationships when the mother must let go and allow the child to seek their own independence, whether the path chosen is at her side or deviant to her teachings and desires.

You are at this very point. You will no longer be indulged. You will be confronted by the consequences of your actions which have led to stagnation, manifesting as "interruptions", and which have led to explosive circumstances, manifesting as "fire".

The phrase "burning bridges" also has a secondary sense. If you burn your bridges, it means that there is no possibility of returning by that same route. This is the quality of your decisions at the present time: they will have permanent consequences which cannot be altered. Burning bridges is only done in situations of desperation. Those with eyes to see will realise that many people, including themselves, find themselves in desperate circumstances, whether this is due to physical loss, losing face, losing friends or relatives, realising that their whole life has been spent doing something illegal or pointless, or whether it is due to succumbing to fear.

These last two situations are the most poignant: if you have spent your precious life in a squandering or poisonous way without knowing it (or even worse, being very well aware of it), then the realization of such will be devastating. Many will see no point in continuing to live because they cannot bear the shame or admit their faults. The same is true for succumbing to fear: through conviction that there is no hope left, many will also fail to continue living.

We talk to you again about these subjects to convey the very grave nature of the very complex situation on earth as it winds down, slower and slower, increasing exposure of this and that atrocity or deception, to develop a pace at which everyone will have the time to attempt to understand. Some people will stick their heads in the sand, of course, but this is only a temporary solution. You will be faced with a lot to digest. You inhabitants of earth will choose how to digest it, assuming you have the ability to do so. Others will just spit it out, not being able to assimilate the truth. Everyone is on their own in this situation, though of course this is also a great opportunity to help those who can let themselves be helped.

This is our message for today. The process is "thickening" and becoming more turgid. The "interruptions" are accumulating fast, and there are more and more bridges burning. We ask you to continue to be well aware of what is happening around you, because you can be sure that you will not be able to anticipate the intensity nor the extreme nature of what awaits you.

Seraphin

Seraphin Message 455:
YOUR CHOICE OF VEHICLE FOR TRAVEL

Through Rosie, 4. August 2021

Dear Inhabitants of Earth: many of you will presently be noticing that you are up against a concrete wall. It is no longer possible to "travel" as you used to, whether this means actual travel to other countries, or movement in other directions, whether this on a physical, material, mental or spiritual level.

You are faced with "interruptions of schedule", with fear, with self-doubt, with the sudden opening up of huge "unheard of" perspectives which you cannot deal with. Faced with such vistas, many close down their minds automatically, claiming that this is not possible. They will strive arduously to deflect new, "outrageous" ideas or revelations. They will be forced to look at many new aspects and to determine whether they are relevant or "true". Many are simultaneously imprisoned in a "mind cage".

Let us take an example here. If someone tells you that the moon is not a piece of rock, caught in earth's orbit, but a large spaceship which has been specifically positioned there to rebalance energies, how will you react? Will you say "Oh, I just saw the moon fly past. Oh no, I was mistaken, it was a bird!" (the art of mockery). Will you say "I love the moon – there are so many wonderful poems written in her honour" (the art of focusing solely on one's own experience). Will you say "You must be some sort of idiot who believes in UFOs" (the art of instant condemnation). Will you say "I think it is time for me to go" (the art of avoidance). Will you say "Yes, yes, there are so many new ideas around at the moment. Have you heard that the earth is flat? (the art of distraction). Or will you say "Now that is an interesting concept: how do you come to that conclusion?"

What is truth?

It is your perception in the moment. One person's truth will most certainly be coloured by their own experience, and will differ from the view of the next person. Much depends on people's choices, and what choice of "vehicle" they have chosen for this experience. With the word "vehicle" we can mean the physical body which one took on at birth, and yes, this was also discussed prior to your incarnation, as the type of body and the sex of the body will determine a great part of your experience. Or we can think of the vehicle as the "cage" of choices you have made in life so far.

To cross difficult terrain, travellers may use a land rover so that they negotiate steep gradients, plunge through rivers and so on. Others who are full of bravado may, for the hell of it, try to negotiate the same stretch of ground in a sports car, with problematic consequences. Some may prefer to walk, taking more time over their journey. Yet other may prefer to take a motorway, whipping past the countryside like a human bullet. Still others will opt to take a plane. This will remove them from the arduous nature of travelling long distances, and may provide an inspiring overview, but the details will be lost.

The real question here is HOW ARE YOU TRAVELLING, or even ARE YOU TRAVELLING AT ALL? If not, perhaps you require a change of vehicle to one which is more appropriate. Whatever the case, it is essential that you conceive of life as a learning journey. Stagnation amounts to death.

In the face of myriad obstacles, such as those presented to you in these end times, what will your decision be? To succumb to paralysis? To run away screaming? To diligently search for loopholes and new opportunities to get things moving? Are you going to be stationary and silenced, beloved citizens of earth, or are you going to rise up, sweeping everything which is lifeless, stagnant, corrupt, futile and damaging in your wake?

With these words, we hope to motivate you out of lethargy and the feeling that you are the victim of "circumstances" with no chance of determining the course of your own fate. Note the power of your thoughts and of your every step. It is up to you to determine how to take that step, and which direction you will take. We are walking alongside you. Seraphin

Seraphin Message 456: TENDING THE INNER GARDEN

Through Rosie, 8th August 2021

Dear Inhabitants of Earth: as we look down on you from our special observation point in space (what you sometimes refer to as "the heavens"), we see that there are so many forlorn souls, like lost sheep. Some are indeed lost, and will later be "repatriated" elsewhere.

You who will remain are actually still on a search for that so-called "heaven". You are convinced that you are far removed from it, that it is very far away and inaccessible, but as with all moments of sudden joyful insight, this "rainbow" is just around the corner, and manifests at that junction when rain and sun are at their strongest, existing simultaneously. Often, a storm is brewing at the same time, symbolic of a great cleansing process. This is where you stand, between two extremes, but there is a beacon of hope, manifesting as a rainbow, and the clouds will, as always, eventually clear. The light wins.

Because most of you have not delved into discovering the perverted depths nor the "heavenly heights" of human experience and beyond (including all humanity's past behaviour, including all humanity's rising and collapsing civilisations), many will feel lost because both ends of the spectrum are such unfamiliar ground. In-depth research into both areas or directions, if you have entered into such, will mean that you will enjoy a comparatively stable stance in view of the shocking revelations to come.

You will have noticed that this is not the first time that we have talked about the "revelations to come", which will indeed stun many due to the fact that they cannot imagine such perfidy, nor the existence of such new, positive and mind-blowing perspectives which will change life for the better.

Faced with all this new information, how will you fare? You may feel lost, as already mentioned. What is the solution to this? How can you deal with it all and still remain sane, developing the desire to make a positive contribution to life on earth, irrespective of the quality of the contribution you have made so far?

The answer my friends is not "blowing in the wind". This answer merely serves to induce hopelessness, lethargy and resignation. The answer lies in TENDING THE INNER GARDEN, and if the inner garden is well tended, the outer garden - which is earth herself – will be abundant also, as one is a reflection of the other. Inner activity translates into outward activity.

If you pour too much water on parched ground after a drought, the water may go to waste, immediately falling down deep cracks. Other plants may suddenly be swamped and cannot deal with it. This means: DO NOT SWAMP YOUR MIND WITH TOO MUCH AT ONCE, for you will not be able to assimilate it. Try to imbibe small pieces of information at a time, digesting them fully.

In a garden which is overgrown, where individual plants may be covered by thorns or vines, it is necessary to do radical clearing work. So it is with rigid, antiquated constructs and deceptive, enslaving belief systems which have taken over your minds. It is necessary to free yourselves of these so that the "inner garden" of your mind is ordered, and so that there is room for new ideas to flourish. It is not enough to do some temporary cosmetic pruning. Parasitical plants must be pulled up by the roots to prevent future destruction and congestion.

A beautiful and attractive garden always requires REGULAR MAINTENANCE and clearing. These are essential actions if you want to have a clear, effective and abundant MIND. If you neglect such duties, other forces will take the opportunity to grow unchecked and will – in the long run – cause havoc.

Havoc is something which has long existed on your planet. It is not simply a state of affairs or a result of circumstance, over which you have no control. It is the EFFECT OF NEGLIGENCE ON A GRAND AND GLOBAL SCALE. AND THIS CAN ONLY BE CORRECTED BY RADICAL MEASURES ON A GRAND AND GLOBAL SCALE.

We cannot go into exactly what measures this will involve, for to do so would take away the learning experience, and there would also be the danger of pre-empting proceedings, which will be in place at exactly the right moment in time. Suffice to say that it is not exactly the right moment to release details. We also note that every individual – according to their own mind-set, expectations and location – will have a different experience, and in some ways, it would therefore be pointless to elaborate. What we can say is that everyone will undergo a great element of surprise, and that everyone will be severely challenged. This is the only possible way forward to counter an extremely severe situation for your earth, and this will happen irrespective of whether you consider your circumstances to be dire or not. We are therefore again here to give you advance warning through the hand of this scribe. Seraphin

Seraphin Message 457: WHAT IS YOUR TRUE IDENTITY?

Through Rosie, 9th August 2021

What is your true identity, Beloveds? In your present society, this subject is much under discussion, and it is inextricably entwined with statements such as YOU MUST RECOGNISE ME AS SUCH AND SUCH, AND THIS IS WHY YOU MUST SHOW ME RESPECT. Yet respect is something which is earned through meritorious behaviour, not simply through association with some disadvantaged marginal group.

Have you understood this fully, Beloveds? (and it is because we love you that we are impelled to bring your attention to such unpleasant topics and why we ask this scribe to put it to paper in the early morning, somewhat against her will).

Can you see the irony of this? IF YOU IDENTIFY, YOU LOSE YOUR IDENTITY AND BECOME AN ITEM IN A GROUP. We use the term "item" here because this is a step towards dehumanization and a step towards destroying one's own sovereignty.

Form your own unique group, consisting of one member only, consisting of your own DIVINE SELF. Do not sacrifice your sovereignty to "feel good", grouping yourselves with others under a restrictive banner. Membership rules of rigid groups means compliance with a certain mind-set and this in turn means a shrinking of spiritual growth. Growing spiritually is your mandate on earth.

We anticipate that there will be many adamant cries as people read this, and of course we recognize that it is a nice feeling to feel "at home" with like-minded people. It may also be very necessary to challenge society on certain issues as a member of such a group. Yet group allegiances should not cloud your vision for truth and should not persuade you to treat deviant behaviour exhibited by fellow group members more lightly. Group member-ship should not override individual sovereignty and decision-making. Neither should it imprison you in a limited capsule of ex-perience. Neither should it exacerbate the feeling that everyone else is your enemy.

If all others are perceived as "enemies" who attack and persecute the group, conflict is pre-programmed and undue sensitivities are ushered in. This can be clearly seen in your present society where much is crushed – especially language – in order to ac-commodate such "sensitivities", and this leads to absurd situa-tions. Your lives are truly out of balance and gravely restricted as a result of the "necessity" to be "politically correct", a position which now stretches across many areas.

Political correctness brings with it an inability to criticize. A critical way of thinking is, however, sorely needed at the present time, if you are not to descend into calamity.

So what is your true identity, Beloveds? You are part of every-thing, and everything is part of you. It is not possible, long-term, to isolate yourselves or separate yourself off.

The next aspect of yourself which we would like to emphasise is that YOU ARE DIVINE. What does this really mean?

IT MEANS THAT YOU ARE SO MUCH MORE THAN A HUMAN PIECE OF MEAT WHICH SUCCUMBS TO MATERIAL AND PHYSICAL DESIRES OR DEMANDS.

INSTEAD, YOU ARE PART OF DIVINE ORDER. YOU HAVE A DIVINE BLUE-PRINT, IN THE SAME WAY THAT EVERY SEED IS DESIGNED TO GROW PERFECTLY IN ACCORDANCE WITH A PERFECT DESIGN.

TO BE DIVINE IS ALSO TO BE
ETERNALLY MOVING FORWARD
ON A LEARNING JOURNEY,
USING WHATEVER "VEHICLE" OR "HUMAN CASING"
YOU HAVE CHOSEN, WITH THE MAIN AIM OF IMPROVING
YOUR QUALITY OF SERVICE TO OTHERS.

To say I AM DIVINE is also to know without a doubt that there is no death – only transition to the next stage. Similarly, there is no "loss", only gaining of experience. There is also NO LIMITATION WITHIN ANY GROUP, just as there is no limitation within any one incarnation: there is only the continued expansion of the SACRED SELF.

We see so many of you stuck in your definitions of yourselves, allowing yourselves to be defined by this or that label, by past "tragedies" or family circumstances, by partners, elders, priests or politicians, but you are none of these definitions. You do not need to sacrifice a part of yourself to the opinions and regulations of others in order to feel WHOLE.

We advise quiet meditation during which you will learn to FEEL the flow of universal love running through your every vein. This is all the support you need – a close connection to the Divine and the secure knowledge that you are part of it. You can ask advice of the Divine in every second. The representatives of the Divine (and this is your mandate also – to represent the Divine more and more each day of your life) in the form of personal unseen guides are always ready to guide and help you. You have but to ask, and we will reply to you. One example of this is these messages which we transfer to the mind of our scribe. She has but to ask a question, and the answer will follow automatically. Writing down the answers is a way of cementing wisdom into your experience. We urge you to develop trust in this process through actual "doing" and experimenting with this. USE THE DIVINE TELEPHONE

SERVICE WHEN YOU ARE IN NEED, rather than retreating in pain to your limited groups which stunt your inner growth by placing you in a supposed but stifling "safe haven".

The real safe haven, however, which stretches throughout eternity, is your own DIVINE CORE. We hope that we have made ourselves clear. If not, we ask you to go within and seek counsel from your DIVINE ADVISORS or your own "HIGHER SELF" which is part of a huge universe, all of which is subject to DIVINE PRINCIPLES, MANIFESTING A PERFECT PLAN IN PERFECTLY ORDERED CYCLES.

For a cycle to close is not a "tragedy" or an "ending", as in the phrase END TIMES which is used deliberately to induce fear and paralysis. Endings are part of a natural and highly intricate mechanism in which each cog is locked into the next, irrespective of whether the cog is small or infinitely large. As already mentioned, you stand on the brink of such a "cycle conclusion", which involves great change. To be intensely aware of your DIVINITY during this phase will be the best way to deal with all that ensues, We embrace you, our DIVINE SUBJECTS*, in our DIVINE ARMS. Seraphin.

*Seraphin wishes to add that the word "subjects" does not imply that you are underlings under celestial control. On the contrary, you are under loving observation and you are subject to our love and guidance, and we try to provide you with our wisdom and overview as necessary.

You are the SUBJECTS, the PRIME MOVERS, and not the victims, in the action which we observe.

Seraphin Message 458:
ONE DROP IN THE OCEAN AND THE POWER OF ONE

Through Rosie, 19th August 2021

Perhaps, Inhabitants of Earth, you are feeling the lowest you have ever been, and perhaps you have never before experienced such depths of helplessness. The absurdity of your existence within the present narrative presented by your media and other "power houses" (a narrative which is always changing in order to make you flounder, as fish caught in a net) is becoming all too clear. You are thrown from side to side, from one fearful scenario to the next: will it be disease, war, nuclear attacks, tornadoes, floods, invasions, rioting or food shortages which afflict you next?

And at the same time, your media stars are perversely providing non-stop theatre called "entertainment" in order to fill any gaps in your fear-filled lives.

There are those, of course, who have little conscience, and who remain unaffected by the real reported "tragedies" which hit others. Yet those reading these messages are seekers, striving to understand and make sense of present circumstances, and their own role in creating them, and how they relate to others.

We see many of you falling into paralysis and helplessness, instead of keeping an objective distance from such reports. We are here to guide you, to show you the way forward, to ease the stagnation, and also – impossible as it might seem – to ignite joy. You will rejoice when you realise that what you have endured in the past will NEVER RETURN ON YOUR WATCH. We say "on your watch", because if you do not continue to be watchful, then such atrocities will repeat themselves.

ARE YOU TRULY HELPLESS, BELOVEDS?

ARE YOU JUST A DROP IN THE OCEAN?

ARE YOU MARCHING THROUGH AN IMPENETRABLE JUNGLE?

You can certainly be compared to a drop of water, and at this juncture it may be worthy to note the following: a drop of water only exists individually when separated out from the ocean, which means that when the drop returns to the ocean, it loses its form and becomes ONE WITH THE WHOLE. It also possesses ALL QUALITIES OF THE WHOLE, and is subject to movement of the whole, and partakes in movement of the whole.

A drop of water may seem to be a tiny, humble, irrelevant and powerless thing, but as part of the whole it is immensely powerful, capable of carving gorges through mountains and changing land-scapes completely, and here we refer also to the "landscape" of the mind.

The "mountain" you are presently staring at is incredibly high. In fact, you do not even comprehend the extent of it, as it stretches beyond the horizon, and the peak is somewhere in the clouds, and you sense that it is completely inaccessible.

The only thing you can do is proceed carefully but firmly, in a direction which you think will benefit you and your fellow humans. This may involve inspiring your fellows to action. It may mean joining in with the worthy project of someone else. It may mean learning a specific skill which you know will come in useful later.

Your decision should not rest on present frameworks or function within presently corrupted practices and power structures. It should be based on what humans need now to truly become

HUMANITY as opposed to existing as automated soulless machines intent on material gain only.

Even if you are in isolation, barred from "society" for your present views, or even if you are banned for your conflicting yet humanity-furthering principles or innovative ideas to correct the situation going further "downhill", do not despair.

REMEMBER THAT YOU ARE
A DROP OF WATER IN THE OCEAN
AND THAT YOU WILL INEVITABLY UNITE WITH
YOUR BROTHERS AND SISTERS TO CREATE
THE ENORMOUS CHANGES WHICH ARE
SO NECESSARY ON THIS EARTH.

REMEMBER ALWAYS THE POWER OF ONE
AND RECOGNISE EVERYTHING
WHICH SEPARATES THE ONE.

If you are but to have one principle to guide you through the trauma of future events, take this as your focus.

IT IS TIME TO UNITE AND SERVE TOGETHER.

YOU WILL BE SERVING THE DIVINE,
WHICH MEANS YOURSELVES, OTHERS, AND ULTIMATELY
THE WHOLE DIVINELY ORCHESTRATED COSMOS.

When everything is falling around your ears,
REMEMBER OUR WORDS AND BE COMFORTED
THAT THIS IS ONLY TEMPORARY.

REMEMBER THAT YOUR INDIVIDUAL EFFORT WILL TURN
IT ALL AROUND FOR THE BETTER.

EVEN A SMALL BOAT CAN CAUSE LARGE WAVES.

YOU ARE SIMULTANEOUSLY ONE DROP OF WATER
AND THE ENTIRE OCEAN.

TOGETHER, YOU CAN FLOAT HEAVY SHIPS,
YOU CAN PUT OUT FIRES,
YOU CAN QUENCH THIRST,
YOU CAN PROVIDE RELIEF FROM HEAT,
YOU CAN GIVE HUMANITY THE
EXPERIENCE OF WEIGHTLESSNESS,
AND YOU CAN INSPIRE EVERYONE
TO KNOW WHAT IT MEANS IS TO BE
TRULY "IN THE FLOW".

MOST IMPORTANTLY, YOU CAN SUSTAIN ALL LIFE AND
YOU CAN REFLECT ALL LIGHT.

We leave this last statement to your own interpretation, but know
that your radiance travels through the universe for millennia.

We walk at your side, Seraphin.

Addendum

A long time ago, this scribe once wrote the following couplet for
a song:

"*One drop in the ocean are you.*
Dreaming alone there's not much you can do".

The answer to your dilemma is DREAMING TOGETHER.

With this thought we leave you, Seraphin

Seraphin Message 459: THE HOLY EXPERIMENT

Through Rosie, 25th August 2021

Dear Inhabitants of Earth: if you were asked to describe the present state of affairs of life on your earth in one sentence, you might say any of the following:

Life is a continuous road of potholes that I try to avoid.

Life is a complete mess, perpetrated by incompetent leaders.

Life is restricted due to rigid government regulations.

Life is a series of mishaps where nobody cares enough.

Life is an endless struggle without any real positive outlook.

Life is a procedure whereby everything steadily goes downhill.

Life is what happens between birth and the grave.

If you are more positive and optimistic, you might say:

Life is a series of ups and downs during which we are challenged to go with the flow.

Life is what we make of it, seizing every opportunity as it arises.

Life is meant for discovering the world and oneself.

Life may be brutal, but we have to make the best of it.

If you have taken up the spiritual path,
you might say the following;

*Life will always present us with
the best opportunity to learn more.*

*Life is something we create personally
through our every decision.*

*Life is a series of progressions during which
we acquire insights and wisdom.*

If you have really understood what is going on here,
you will say:

LIFE IS A HOLY EXPERIMENT,
SPECIFICALLY DESIGNED BY THE ANGELIC REALMS,
CELESTIAL UNIVERSE ADMINISTRATION
AND COSMIC INTELLIGENCE,
TO SET US FIRMLY UPON THE PATH OF
SPIRITUAL EVOLUTION WITH THE AIM OF DISCOVERING
AND LIVING OUR MISSION IN SERVICE TO OTHERS AND
EVERYONE ELSE IN THE COSMOS.

Do you see where this is going, Beloveds? Can you see where
all your conventional learning lessons, presented by faulty and
censored textbooks in your schools, have missed the point completely? Can you see how you have been indoctrinated to think
that your "career" is purely an earthly, material and materialistic
affair?

Can you grasp that there is a HOLY plan, and that you are an integral part of it, however "small" you may consider yourself? Even the largest of complicated machines requires one single, small IGNITION, and you can see yourselves as such catalysts for the manifestation of GREAT VISIONS which are to come.

So, the next question is: are you going to rise to the occasion, or are you going to reject this information and retire into your comfortable cages, enclosed in your mind-prisons? Time is getting short, and your decisions are crucial.

The "holy experiment" here on earth is an era of dispensation, during which you have been allowed to take your time, to wander at will, to leave the spiritual path and go in the opposite direction for hundreds of years, if not longer, and in this, your celestial rulers have been extremely tolerant, understanding your motives, your reasoning, your excuses and your lethargy. However, you are now at the end of the course. The era of dispensation, where everything is allowed, is coming to an end.

You have been given myriad opportunities. You have been presented with wisdom and insight by numerous incognito members of the celestial hierarchy who have incarnated among you. You have been given the benefit of the doubt, and you have been able to experience a whole variety of "ups and downs" of which the members of the celestial hierarchy – in the final analysis – highly disapprove, yet they held a glimmer of hope for you, hoping that you would one day turn, even at the very last moment, towards the light.

That moment has come and gone. There will be no more chances. There will now be assessment and adjudication. We urge you to prepare yourselves mentally for this.

Seraphin

Seraphin Message 460: WE ASK FORGIVENESS

Through Rosie, 28th August 2021

Dearly beloved Inhabitants of Earth. During these momentous times in your physical reality, we have tried to provide you with information and insights which may act as a point of light in the darkness. Yet the darkness is so dense that it has not been easy to provide an overview. Neither would it have been wise to shower you with intricate details of the most horrendous crimes which have been committed, for to do so would have been to shock you into silence, to cause paralysis, and even to cause your demise and death. (Your safety might also have been impaired, for knowledge is power, and power is a threat to those who already hold power and do not want to let go).

This we cannot do. It would not have served the greater cause. The carriers of truth – who are YOURSELVES – must be preserved and aided in a way which optimally supports you on your path. This does not include information overload as much as providing guidance regarding behaviour according to cosmic law. It is such behaviour which will perpetrate peace. Thus, we have been feeding you specific "titbits", rather than offering you an entire 3-course meal.

When all this is over – and you will be in no doubt when this happens – you will be devastated when you realise the amount of information we have kept from you. We have also hinted at cosmic perspectives, and at the significance of the process of spiritual upliftment which is earth's goal, but you have little concept of the ramifications of this, or of the opportunities it opens up for other parts of the universe. Let us say that your "spectrum of experience" will widen greatly in all directions – ranging from the depths of despair to the heights of ecstasy.

Some of you may turn around with anger saying WHY DID YOU NOT TELL US MORE? If you go back to previous messages, you will find hints of what is to be revealed, but you will not find the entire picture. We have provided you with our reasons for this – to prevent you from being overwhelmed, and to allow the mission to continue, and to ensure an excellent and appropriate pace of learning, yet at the same time our hearts have been very heavy, and we have suffered knowing that you do not know all.

We also know that the sudden shock of knowing may cause some to pass from this world. Thus, we are at the same time full of hope and joy, and full of regret for your suffering. This has been a "lesson in a rarefied space", rather than a lesson in brute reality. It is as if you have been living in a "time warp" which now needs to be brought "up to speed". And so, though we are fully aware of the import of our mission, and though nothing will sway us from our course, and although joy and peace will be yours in the end, we ask forgiveness for the nature of the lesson which has had to be adapted to the setting of classroom earth, so that learning can best proceed. We love you, Seraphin.

Seraphin Message 461: THE NEW SPIRITUAL LIFE

Through Rosie, 17th September 2021

Beloved Citizens of Earth:
The "new spiritual life" you will be moving towards is one which is characterized by CLOSENESS. (Unfortunately, your present civilization is characterized by SEPARATION).

Only by close observance of past failures, as well as of one's own faulty behaviour which has led to devastating results, will the situation be capable of redemption. The cult of individuality has reached its peak, and this is a lobby which furthers selfishness, the desire to "live it up" and "not miss out", take what it may. You crave the feeling of having no regrets. You exploit every opportunity ruthlessly so that in the end, you can proudly say that you have really LIVED.

But is this really the case? One might have had all sorts of exciting physical experiences or travels, but the inner journey may be in complete stagnation, and this is what we would like to draw your attention to today. For those who have indulged in all sorts of excesses, in order to really FEEL that they are enjoying life to the full, we would advise that there is a completely different world of "feeling" which is available to you, if you open up to it. And this far surpasses the temporary thrills, the intense rides, the highs which, when they are over, will send you into another "low", leaving you stranded and desperate to relive the high again.

The truly spiritual life involves a constant seam of joy running through your daily actions, an all-pervading calm which allows you to take a deep breath before plunging into any automatic reaction, a sensitivity which allows you to put yourself always and completely in the shoes of another, sensing the joys and also the pains of their mental and physical landscape as intimately as if they were your own.

Contrast all this with your present society and lamentable levels of compassion and awareness, and it will be all too clear to you that you have entered an abyss. For some people, it is an abyss of no return, despite the helping hands we have so often offered. The planet has yet again entered a very "dark age", and as everything becomes more absurd and more turgid, coming inevitably to stagnation and standstill, many will simply succumb to fear and desperation, for they do not see any "light" on the horizon, and neither do they comprehend that they themselves are the "light" which can penetrate this darkness.

Others will shut their eyes. They lack the steadfastness, integrity and courage to face that which they have collectively created, however unwittingly.

So it has come to this, inhabitants of earth, that you who have an inkling of the seriousness of these circumstances will be the ones who rise up and shake the earth into new beginnings. This will be a very difficult undertaking, requiring the intense and dedicated effort of thousands if not millions. Those who are a burden to earth and who cannot conceive of their responsibilities or their potential will leave to repeat those lessons somewhere else.

The spiritual life is one where attention is paid
to both physical processes and inner processes,
one being a reflection of the other.

THE MAIN MOTIVATION GUIDING THE SPIRITUAL LIFE IS
THAT OF UPLIFTING THE PLANETARY VIBRATIONS
AND THE VIBRATIONS OF EVERYTHING AND EVERYONE
ON THE PLANET.

There are no exceptions to this. There are no "days off" or times when this does not apply. Similarly, there are no occasions on which something does not matter. Every detail matters for all eternity.

The second guiding principle of the spiritual life is the acute awareness of unification. Every thought is part of a unified consciousness, and every thought affects the quality and extent of that unified consciousness. To be fully aware of the effect of one's thoughts and actions at every moment is the attribute of a truly spiritually-led life. This applies not only to unified families, communities or nations, but to the whole planet, and in fact the whole cosmos, of which a huge part is as yet unknown to you. But still, you are connected and affect each other.

Thus we of the celestial administration, however far away our observation point, and however "different" we may seem to be to you in thought or form, will always be part of you and will always affect your destiny.

Our presence here at this critical time is
PART OF OUR SPIRITUAL LIFE.
We are here to assist and to make you aware of the
GREATER WHOLE, and that
WE ARE ALL PART OF DIVINE MACHINATIONS.

The time draws closer when those who are capable of being awakened to such truths will actually be given the proof which will catapult them onto a new level, making these new insights possible, and thus making a new spiritual life possible.

This level of spiritual living is a REQUIREMENT for continuing on this earth. While earth has tolerated much which is not in alignment with her wishes, she is now moving forward with our help, and moving forward always includes a measure of "letting go" of that which does not serve.

Thus, much will be released,
including those who do not actively support Earth.
This means supporting her HEALTH AND ABUNDANCE.

This means solving conflicts and disallowing violence on her soil.
This means showing her LOVE for at every possible juncture.

To those who are capable of this we say COME!
WE WILL BUILD A WONDERFUL FUTURE TOGETHER.

We are ready to help and support you on this path.

Seraphin

Seraphin Message 462: THE UNLIMITED LIFE

Through Rosie, 26th September 2021

Never assume, Beloveds, that there are any limitations.
I am instructing this scribe to relate a recent experience,
in order to illustrate this:

*"I was staying at a farm, surrounded by hens, dogs, cats and a
goat. Sometimes the hens and the goat would manage to escape
from their pen, and the border collie would stalk them and prevent
them from going further afield. A fence ran around the property
also, to keep them in, and in this fence was a small, decorative
gate. On the other side, there was a lush green property with attractive water channels. I looked longingly over the fence and
wondered who it all belonged to. One morning I awoke to see the
fleeting figure of a child on a bicycle moving towards the gate.
Then I heard the squeak of the gate opening. I was completely
shocked. The garden beyond the gate was not a specially cor-
doned off and "out of bounds" area, but a path used daily to go
to school. I could have gone through the gate at any time. Seeing
the child go through, I did not hesitate to do the same and found
areas which contrasted wildly with my imaginings."*

As you can see from this simple example, limitations are blockages which you have created in your own mind due to psycho-
logical patterns of thinking which have been set in place by those
who wish to control.

The most effective way of controlling you is to maintain "fences"
and to induce fear, cutting you off from your divine centre, from
your divine intuition, from divine guidance and from your own
divinity per se.

You have been persuaded – under a sort of mass hypnosis – that divinity (or GOD, as you often call it) is mysteriously SOMEWHERE ELSE, is mysteriously INACCESSIBLE and is mysteriously CRUEL, and that it will DISPENSE PUNISHMENT AT THE SLIGHTEST DEVIATION FROM THE SCRIPT.

This keeps you obediently in your place. This results in a stunted and regulated life, lived according to a given framework, as opposed to a fluid, forward-moving and exhilarating experience which you create yourselves, stepping lightly with exuberance through a life full of divine ecstasy.

The time has come when you are being given the opportunity to RECOGNISE THE FENCES YOU FALSELY REVERE, AND TO OPEN THE GATES WHICH YOU HAVE NOT DARED TO OPEN.

Indeed, you might have seen such gates, and you may have admired their beauty, but you have not conceived of their real purpose. You have considered them decorative, an appendage to the scene, part of the landscape offering a measure of protection, but you have not realised that they are a gateway to new experiences, or that they are in fact unlocked, and you have never even tried to open the latch.

Neither have such gateways been held in your awareness. If you had been observing closely, you would have seen (as this scribe saw) the gate being used by others on a daily basis. You have been grossly deceived, little ones, lulled into a sense of security that this is how it should be, that "perfection" or "satisfaction" or "high standards" have already been reached, and that it would be pointless or ungrateful to strive for more.

So thoroughly have you let yourselves be duped, citizens of earth. It is time to re-examine your lives and your surroundings and circumstances closely, find that door and open it, rejoicing in the new horizons which result from traversing a new landscape. We encourage you to do this on a physical and mental level, for much "confinement" has been imposed upon you in recent times, and much of that "confinement" has been construed to turn you into slaves, or rather to continue your already existing slavery with a different twist.

You can imagine the trauma when the "doors" open unexpectedly of their own accord, by celestial order. It will serve you to explore in advance so that you do not find yourselves among those who cannot bear the knowledge that they have been enslaved, in accordance with their own wish and agreement, and that this appalling condition could have been ended at any time, not by celestial order but by THEMSELVES.

This message intends to lessen this burden. If heeded, it will do so. We suffer with those who suffer, and it is this which impels us to talk to you today. Seraphin.

Seraphin Message 463:
THE IMPORTANCE OF SURRENDER

Through Rosie, 30th September 2021

It is time to pay very careful attention, beloved Inhabitants of Earth. We have often said that your world will turn "upside down", and thus it goes without saying that the various concepts you cherish, as well as various usages of diverse terms which you favour, will be shattered or shown to mean something completely different from what you actually thought. One such term is the word SURRENDER.

What is surrender? Surrender is not defeat, but chosen alignment with the Divine. For many on earth, to surrender means to be weak, to give in, to stop fighting, to surrender to the enemy. It is, in your minds, a shameful and sinful necessity, during which one sacrifices one's ideals, loyalties and convictions. This is the connotation you carry after centuries of warring and forcing each other to your knees, and much worse. In the past, those who were forced to surrender were subjected to every kind of violence, rape and death. It was a progression, on your earth plane, when prisoners were not shot or eaten, but taken away as slaves. That this was actually a progression in your behaviour shows you how long and tedious your progress has been over the ages, and indeed, it is not over yet, as wars still spawn across earth's soil at an alarming rate today.

Thus, you are convinced that surrendering is a BAD THING during which you are stripped of dignity, honour and freedom. YET IT IS THE EXACT OPPOSITE.

We are not talking here about taking part in warfare and having to put down arms.

We are talking about RECOGNISING ULTIMATE WISDOM
AND ALIGNING ONESELF WITH THAT WISDOM
IN ORDER TO BETTER SERVE HUMANITY.
And as part of humanity yourselves,
you will of course also benefit.

Does this sound like SACRIFICE?
Like giving something up?
Like no longer being able to do what you want?

In a way, this is true, yet the baubles and petty entertainments you cling to are vastly inferior to the joys you will experience when you embrace surrender to divine wisdom and cosmic law. Your previous pastimes will appear to you like lustreless baubles on a tree in comparison with the rich and deep encounters which are a result of such alignment. You will, in effect, live in continuous joy, instead of navigating the "ups and downs" of a directionless existence.

We would like to expand more on the word "direction". If you know 100 percent that the direction you are following will have a pleasant and successful outcome, why would you not follow it or "succumb" or "surrender" to it? Following cosmic law is following a DIVINE DIRECTION. It cannot fail. There are no disappointments (What you give, you receive, as being one example of unfailing cosmic law). Similarly, there are no loopholes or exceptions, and it is not possible to simply take a detour or wander off the path, for this will put your future experiences in jeopardy. Quite simply, you have the choice whether to move in a worthy direction, or whether to wander haphazardly, drifting with a feeling of hopelessness.

Have you ever experienced true surrender, Beloveds?

There are some states of being which may give you an idea of what true surrender feels like. The first is floating in water. The water represents nature loving you, moving without hesitation into every crevice, filling every space between your toes and fingers, seeping into every pore. It does not ask questions. It does not make demands. It does not sign a contract with you. It just flows, and it carries you on buoyant waves. It is possible to float in a completely relaxed position, releasing all, feeling weightless. You are not on the lookout for drops of water which might hurt you, exploit you, demand your attention or cause you stress. You are simply accepting nature's love.

The second state of being is the moment before you fall asleep. You (hopefully) have had enough to eat, your physical needs have been taken care of, you lie in a warm bed, you (hopefully) feel calm and full of gratitude, YOU STOP TALKING AND SUR-RENDER YOURSELF TO SLEEP. This you do on a daily basis, Beloveds, yet this state of being is also required of you during the day. We will name some examples.

SURRENDER IS REQUIRED IF YOU ARE GOING TO LEARN

We can say that there is so much that you will have to learn on this planet, because you are very backward in your level of spirituality. It is absolutely NECESSARY that you recognize your IGNORANCE and that you SUCCUMB TO THE WISDOM OF THE ELDERS AND TEACHERS WHO WILL APPEAR BEFORE YOU. This requires you to dismiss the ego. This requires you also to dismiss all feelings of shame at past mistakes. This requires you to get over the feeling of "losing face". Especially – but not only – in the eastern hemispheres of your world, this is a major problem. To pretend to know, when one does not, is a major flaw. To be full of bravado, when one is not, is another major flaw. To admit that one has much to learn is a major virtue. To be eager to know the truth will spur you on to discover principles and qualities which – if adopted by all – will transform your global society.

SURRENDER IS REQUIRED
IF YOU ARE GOING TO WORK TOGETHER.

There can be no more statements of "I am better than you". There can be no more battles to climb ladders independently, elbowing others out of the way. It will be your mandate to pool intelligence and ideas to produce the very best result. This will often mean holding your tongue and letting another speak. This will mean developing patience. This will mean listening to experts as they offer advice. This also means that whatever the project, or whatever the organization, it must SURRENDER TO A DIVINE CAUSE. It cannot simply exist for the fun of it, for making the most money possible, or for exploiting earth's resources to produce cheap and unnecessary goods. It must have a mission, and all persons involved in this mission must have the mission at heart as opposed to self-interest. Self-interest is secondary.

SURRENDER IS REQUIRED
FOR PERFECT BALANCE AND CONTINUOUS JOY.

Conjure up, if you will, the image of two children on a seesaw. If they are both going to enjoy the ride, then there must be regular and rhythmic give and take, a regular exchange of energy, a regular pulsing of opposites, a continuous alternation between giving a boost and surrendering to the boost that the other person provides.

SURRENDER IS REQUIRED FOR LASTING PEACE
BETWEEN INDIVIDUALS AND NATIONS.

To continuously rehash old complaints, debts or "chips on one's shoulder" (and you are always at least 50% responsible anyway), is to constantly bring the pot to the boil and to make one's counterpart constantly rise in defence. The solution to this is working on oneself, realizing how one's own negative behaviour contributed to these issues.

THIS INVOLVES FORGIVING ONESELF AND OTHERS.
THIS MEANS SURRENDERING ONE'S SUPPOSED RIGHT
TO COMPLAIN. IT INVOLVES CHOOSING TO SURRENDER
IN FAVOUR OF THE GREATER HARMONY OF THE WHOLE,
RATHER THAN CHOOSING TO PROMULGATE CONFLICT.

Again, this does not actually mean ignoring or glossing over unpleasant realities. It means releasing old behavioural patterns which ultimately do not serve you personally, or your society, or your nation.

SURRENDER IS REQUIRED TO NURTURE THE HEALTH OF YOUR HOSTESS, THE EARTH.

Without this, you will not survive. You will have to surrender your squandering lifestyles, your "I couldn't care less" attitudes, and your inattention to environmental matters and sustainability.

SURRENDER IS REQUIRED
IN ALL RELATIONSHIPS AND ALL COUPLINGS.

Regarding men and women, they are unique, and uniquely different. They cannot vie. Neither can either "win". No man or woman can EVER be better than their partner, or put themselves above their partner, if they intend the relationship to be a success. Their decisions will always be for the good of themselves as a couple, as opposed to themselves as an individual. And as a couple, they will also have a mission which they will personally define, and which will not be restricted to selfish aims. This does not mean sacrificing certain interests or skills. It means using those skills to achieve something wonderful together which will benefit others, manifesting a way of relating to each other which others can emulate. You will be role models for each other, in whatever combination, in whatever working relationship. If this degree of surrender of a purely personal direction is accomplished, there will be a massive synergy effect which cannot be achieved by one person alone, and which is way beyond your imagination.

The classic example of this is the conductor and an orchestra. All the musicians are professional, capable of playing as soloists, and every instrument is different, with various timbres and tones:

YET THEY ALL FOLLOW THE SAME SCRIPT,
THEY ALL LISTEN TO EACH OTHER INTENTLY,
AND THEY ALL SURRENDER IN ORDER TO
PRODUCE A HARMONIOUS WHOLE.

A musician or a singer in a choir must always hold back, perform when it is their turn, and attune themselves to their fellow musicians. If someone "turns rogue" and fails to do this, the whole piece of music is ruined. With this we wish to emphasise the unique playing potential of every individual in creating a new and harmonious society on earth. If you have not already done so, you will realise that this sort of new direction is sorely needed.

Rather than being a burden,
SURRENDERING IS LIBERATING.

It is not just one person – you – who are asked to surrender, but EVERYONE. This means that the playing field is levelled. There may still be leaders and organisers and conductors, but there is mutual respect. This means the end of harassment, bullying, exploitation and arrogance. To surrender is to further spiritual principles, to support the spiritual life (which we have mentioned in an earlier message), and to gloriously co-create a future pervaded by a feeling of equality and love.

And here we come to the crux of the matter:
SURRENDERING IS DEMONSTRATING LOVE
for something greater than yourselves.

It is giving up the old and striving for a better path. It is knowing that every step taken carefully will contribute to a wonderful solution. Surrendering one's own crusted, irrelevant and twisted viewpoint, and viewing everything from a neutral position, will open up vistas of potential.

For many, this will not be easy. You will have to surrender your erroneous views, your erroneous religious convictions, your debilitating ideas about life and death, your corrupted senses of identity and your inaccurate history. All will fall.

What will you do then, Beloveds? Will you wail and flail around with your hands, lamenting that the nightmare has come to an end? Will you be able to let it go? Will you even be able to recognize that it was a nightmare, and that momentous changes need to be made?

When all this has fallen, you may feel desolate. You may feel empty, but it is this very moment of emptiness and surrender which enables you to be filled by love, and this is the essential element which should guide your steps in the future.

You will SURRENDER TO THE WORDS OF YOUR HEART.

You will learn to align yourselves with the heart. You will succumb to her advice. You will let her take the lead. And thus you will jointly flood your world with loving kindness. All actions which do not fit into this category will no longer be tolerated.

We hope that we have given you some insight into the importance of surrender. Without it, you will remain dishonest, instable, backward individuals and nations who run the risk of repeating the dreadful experience you are now having.

This will no longer be permitted by the celestial hierarchy which observes you and which will, when the time comes, openly guide you.

Our work here is also characterised by surrender. It is our personal will to uplift and enlighten you wayward ones on planet earth, and while there are cosier and pleasanter jobs to be had, we choose to enter into this scenario because love prompts us to do so.

Seraphin.

Seraphin Message 464:
THE IMPORTANCE OF SURRENDER TO DIVINE TIMING

Through Rosie, 2nd October 2021

As an addendum to the previous message on surrender, we would like to further address an important aspect which has not yet been covered enough. This is the concept of DIVINE TIMING. It is actually not a concept at all.

IT IS REALITY.

YOUR LIVES ARE DIVINELY GUIDED.

THE QUESTION IS: DO YOU REALISE THIS?

DO YOU SURRENDER TO THIS DIVINE GUIDANCE?

Do you find time to sit in quiet meditation, clear your mind and ask the divine core within yourself for advice? And if something unpleasant or disappointing occurs, blocking your most favoured path, shattering your dreams and leaving you reeling in shock, can you accept that such obstacles are also the actions of DIVINE HAND in an attempt to stop you moving towards disaster, or to encourage you to move in a direction more worthy?

Are barriers actually a sign of assistance?
Can you SURRENDER to the fact that this is not the right time, or perhaps the right place, to do what you had planned?

This ties in with the fact that you all have a specific task to fulfil on earth – a task which was discussed and decided previous to your incarnation here. You are always being assisted by unseen guides (which are REPRESENTATIVES OF THE DIVINE, working for the DIVINE) in order to fulfil that mandate. They are the ones who place the obstacles, the ideas and the opportunities.

This turns life into an adventure. The smallest or the largest occurrence could be a sign pointing you in the DIVINE DIRECTION. It is up to you to SUCCUMB AND SURRENDER to this Divine guidance in order to live a truly fulfilling and beneficial life. If things do not turn out as you wish, or if something does not happen on your own timing, then you can be sure that the DIVINE has other plans for you, and that there are still other issues to be looked at, or problems to be solved, or knots which need untying, or issues which require closure, before that particular avenue is open to you.

This is valid on a personal level and also a global level. Many of you who are "in the know" about the DIVINE DESTINY of this planet have been impatient with the "wrapping up" of the old, corrupt age, and are eager to move on to the new. And we say: ALL IN GOOD TIMING, which means ALL IN DIVINE TIMING. We encourage you to think more along these lines, and to make good use of the time which is left to you, because it affords you an unparalleled opportunity to learn. We again take our leave, Seraphin

SERAPHIN MESSAGE 465:
THE IMPORTANCE OF SURRENDER
IN CREATING THE SACRED

Through Rosie, 7th October 2021

We would like to continue, Beloveds on Earth, with our instructions concerning surrender – a word which instantly triggers many of you because you feel it involves SACRIFICE. (And it is of course always your choice whether to work on yourselves, thus removing the trigger, or whether to avoid working on yourselves and simply remove the word). In a way, it does involve sacrifice, yet the OUTCOME of surrendering is vastly preferable to the chaos and enslavement which you have generated on your earth today. As we have already mentioned, surrender is a method of increasing your joy and serenity.

INSTRUCTIONS FOR A PEACEFUL AND JOYFUL LIFE:

IT IS NECESSARY TO SURRENDER FIXED IDEAS.
A FIXED IDEA IS FINITE.
A FIXED IDEA LIMITS YOU.

If you release a fixed idea, you open up the door to growth. You allow EVEN GREATER VISIONS TO BLOOM. Why would you want to limit yourselves, Beloveds? Why would you encourage restricting, enslaving and unsatisfactory conditions when you could be leading projects which have a huge capacity to impact large numbers of people positively?

Would this not be SACRED WORK?

You must SURRENDER your ideas of "me as opposed to you" and of "my success" and "my goal". You must release the focus on yourself and start to INCLUDE OTHERS IN YOUR TRAIN OF THOUGHT. You must release ideas of personal gain, personal wealth and personal steps up the career ladder, and you must start to see yourself IN RELATION TO ALL OTHERS AND ALL THINGS, positioning yourself and your contributions IN COMBI-NATION with other contributions so that a synergy effect can take place, resulting in a huge explosion of potential.

To harbour secrets and to "opt out" of this communal forward movement is to miss out on fulfilment. To withdraw, and to avoid participation, is to cement your own unhappiness. Do you have a pet project or a pet plan? Are you proud of being the instigator of such a plan? If so, you must SURRENDER YOUR SUPPOSED OWNERSHIP, FOR NOTHING SACRED WILL BE ACHIEVED IN COMPLETE ISOLATION.

You need others to GROW AND LEARN FASTER, Beloveds, and we can say that although there have been some very fast learners on your earth plane, the majority have been PLODDING ALONG AT AN INCREDIBLY SLOW RATE. These are the ones for whom surrender is a difficult concept, for they already consider themselves as victims who have "surrendered". These are the ones who, for the most part, refuse to learn and who will reap the (unfortunately negative) results of their (unfortunately negative) behaviour. Know also that we love these "little ones", who cannot conceive of their own greatness and potential, and that is why we try to reach them through such messages.

Coming back to the title of this piece: it is your personal mandate to CREATE SOMETHING SACRED – not something which is flighty, temporary, mundane or mediocre. It should be characterised by EXCELLENCE. It might have a stunning effect on others, assisting their growth and lighting up their faces with amazement at such beauty, or it may instigate a longing for peace, or it may instil them with increased sensitivity, or it may dispel their greatest fears, or it may fill them with gratitude, or it may bring them to a place of calm, content in the knowledge that they are supported, loved and cared for.

ALL WORK ON EARTH FALLS INTO
ONE OF THESE CATEGORIES,
AND IF CARRIED OUT WITH DEVOTION,
DILIGENCE AND ATTENTION TO DETAIL,
IT WILL BE SACRED WORK.

We would like to focus on one particular category. The most sacred of tasks, in which SURRENDER plays a never-ending and pivotal role, is that of raising children. Not a second goes by, in the heart of a true parent, which is not used for the teaching of the child, and, by the same token, of the child teaching the parent how to teach. The child, in order to learn, must surrender to the knowledge and wisdom of the parent, and the parent must surrender to the slower pace and not-yet-developed learning capacities of the child. Parents are required to be constantly patient and to constantly adjust themselves. Nothing can be forced. There is a phrase which says "Don't cut off a piece bigger than you can swallow". All processes must be thorough, constant and appropriate to the "digestive system" of the "swallower".

What if your present occupation is LESS THAN SACRED? This is an excellent time to review your activities, looking at them from this aspect. We hope that we have been able to provide you with some insights which will serve you and everyone in the future. Seraphin.

Seraphin Message 466: THE FINAL CURTAIN

Through Rosie, 27th October 2021

Are you aware that you are watching a very intricate and well-structured play, Beloveds, with plots and subplots, with misleading decoys, with a host of deceptive moves and twists to the story which keep you on the edge of your seats? If the actors are doing their job well, then you will enter fully into this illusion, which in this case is also a DELUSION, forgetting everything and everyone around you. You will regard it all as "real".

The measure of the skill of the actors can only be truly determined at the very end of the play WHEN THE FINAL CURTAIN FALLS. If you have been completely engrossed in all this "make believe", you will be completely in shock when it ends; you will be stuck in a state of "suspending disbelief", still completely identifying with the protagonists, believing that their script is their own, sympathizing with their ups and downs, celebrating their successes and commiserating with the failures of their endeavours.

You may even be in tears because the situations portrayed were so violent, so moving, so frightening and so lifelike, yet with one huge jolt you will suddenly realise THAT THIS WAS ONLY A SHOW, INTENDED PURELY TO ENTERTAIN YOU, TO KEEP YOU BUSY, TO STOP YOU CONCENTRATING ON MORE IMPORTANT THINGS. MOST IMPORTANT OF ALL, IT HAS DRAWN YOUR ATTENTION AWAY FROM THE TRUTH.

At this stage, inhabitants of earth, you may still be asleep, you may still be worried by the "action" in the play, and you may ask WHAT TRUTH?

We would answer:

THE TRUTH OF WHAT REALLY LIES AROUND YOU,
AND THE TRUTH THAT
YOU HAVE COLLECTIVELY CREATED IT,
AND THAT THESE DEPLORABLE CIRCUMSTANCES
CANNOT ANY MORE BE BORNE BY YOUR EARTH
WHO DIRECTLY FEELS EVERY NEGATIVE THOUGHT,
AND WHO IS SERIOUSLY BURDENED
BY EVERY NEGATIVE ACT.

Perhaps you do not yet realise how long this has been going on, for you assess the situation only as you know it from your experiences during your own lifetime. Yet this negativity has been accumulating for thousands and thousands of years. You are used to such a negative atmosphere. You have been fed bad news from your rogue media your entire lives. Those that pull the strings have put on an excellent show in order to keep you in your seats, to control you, to ensure that you have no time or capacity to think for yourselves. They have fed you an exciting and riveting narrative, and the majority have come to believe that this narrative is true. Nothing has been big or strong enough to challenge it. Those who have tried have been for the most part silenced.

Yet you vastly underestimate what has been going on behind the scenes. This "play" is not restricted to the global "theatre hall". Not only have YOU been onlookers of this play, but many other off-planet observers have been watching the plot thicken – again for thousands of years – because they are so concerned about your gullibility. They see the "play" from a completely different angle. They see the global spectators being grossly deceived to the point that they stare – zombie-like – at nothing but the designated stage. They never leave their seats, even if invited out for a break. Their eyes do not leave the stage for one second. All the greater will be the shock, Beloveds, when the play unexpectedly ends, and the curtain falls.

Many will scream OH NO! IT CAN'T JUST END LIKE THIS! Others will be completely paralysed. They will not be able to leave their seats. Yet others will shout in anger or cry bitter tears. Some will die of fear, for their world has collapsed. Some will stubbornly refuse to leave, convinced that the curtain will rise again, and that the play will continue. YET EVERYONE MUST LEAVE THAT THEATRE HALL and everyone will be forced to reflect on the meaning of the play. You may feel dejected, disappointed, deceived and alone. You may "lose face" for having put so much energy into identifying with the characters who – it is now obvious to you – were part of an evil faction intending to lead you away from assessing and preventing all sorts of criminal activity. You will realise that the actors were the willing or unwitting minions of those whose sole intention it was to deceive and enslave you. This will be your major wake-up call:

YOU WILL REALISE THAT YOU HAVE BEEN SLAVES,
AND THAT YOUR ATTENTION, YOUR STRENGTHS
AND IN FACT YOUR DIVINE POTENTIAL
HAVE BEEN HELD CAPTIVE FOR MILLENNIA.

The shock of this cannot be underestimated. Many will not survive it, and especially those who have deliberately partaken in evil rituals and activities will not survive, for they will be truly exposed as "only actors in a play", and a very evil play at that, when the FINAL CURTAIN FALLS.

Those who can cope with this scenario, who can enter a state of humility, as well as of wonder, and who are able to master the very steep learning curve which approaches, will be supported and assisted in their recovery and in their future endeavours. You will not be left alone, Citizens of Earth, to wallow pitifully in the dreadful "aftermath". Celestial help will be forthcoming, but this will not be a constant shower of indications about where to go and what to do. The most successful evolution of mind takes place when individuals take their own initiative, go through their own experiences, and build their own paradises, step by step. We are here to act as a catalyst, to inspire and to guide this process, and we shall not fail you.

Many preparations for your future voyage – as major protagonists – are already in place. We have been working steadily behind the scenes while your attention has been on the show. Those of you who have already detected flaws in the plot, or disconnect in the proceedings, or weakness in the acting abilities of those on stage, will be better prepared for the revelation that all this "holds no water". We ask you to be strong and to support those who are left desperate and dumfounded when the curtain falls. Guide them out of the dark theatre into the light, and help them discover a new world compassed by divine principles and fuelled by unconditional love. This is what we want to impress on you today, Beloveds, FOR THIS TIME IS APPROACHING.

Seraphin.

Seraphin Message 467: A WORD OF ENCOURAGEMENT

Through Rosie, 30th October 2021

Today we would like to give a word of encouragement to those who are depressed, downhearted or desperate, and who can see no way out of this labyrinth of disasters and corruption, for you are walking as if the sun has been extinguished, yet all the darkness of your little world is not capable of distancing you from the all-pervasive, infinite and eternal LIGHT OF THE COSMOS WHICH PENETRATES ALL.

What is this "light" you may ask, for in your present experience of darkness, it is very difficult to imagine the opposite. Indeed, it has been a deliberate strategy in some cases, to allow you to experience "dark times" in order to come to the final realization that this is not a worthy path to pursue.

Imagine that a space craft picks you up and takes you to a planet where the inhabitants are vastly superior in their spiritual evolution. Imagine suddenly landing in areas of exquisite beauty, both natural and "human-made", which abound throughout the planet without even one smirch on the face of this beauty. Imagine being immersed in immense kindness every minute of the day, showered with love by every stranger, treated with respect at every turn, allowed to express yourself fully at every opportunity, encouraged to grow into the most glorious version of yourself whenever possible. And all this while you are in a state of continuous joy, without stress or worries of any kind.

How will you feel, Beloveds, after having experienced EXACTLY THE OPPOSITE on earth, where you have been moulded into slaves, subjected to unbending rules, forced to consume tainted food and medication without your knowledge, coerced into succumbing to all power, forced to live in crowded, unhygienic and polluted environments, subjected to continuous noise, corrupted by false teachings and forced to forget completely YOUR OWN DIVINITY. What if you suddenly started to regard each other as DIVINE BEINGS, which indeed many of you are?

This is the light of which we speak.
THE LIGHT WHICH FIRES YOUR SOUL, WHICH EXPANDS YOU AND INSPIRES YOU WITH ENDLESS OPTIMISM, WHICH FUELS YOUR LOVE FOR HUMANITY, WHETHER ON THIS PLANET OR THE NEXT.

There are no limits to love; its positive vibration travels at more than the speed of light across the universes.
It is unstoppable, it is powerful, it can never be quenched.

This is what is so sadly lacking on your sorry planet where hatred, fear, sadness and violence have caught foothold, and have prevailed for centuries and beyond. You have been unable – despite the attempts of many "masters" who have come to ENLIGHTEN YOU, to throw off these shackles and BE THE LIGHT.

Yet although this may seem to be an interminably long time of "darkness" to you, this is only a temporary situation in the history of the universes. One great truth which has been kept from you at all costs is the existence of the REST OF THE COSMOS, which is huge and organized.

Just as your earth is divided into countries with administrations, so are the millions of planets organised and under administrative rule. You might like to call this UNDER HEAVEN'S RULE or UNDER CELESTIAL RULE, but generally you are so unused to using such vocabulary and to hearing about such concepts.

Suffice to say that the celestial administration is grounded in love and that it has one purpose: to regulate and restrain "evil" and to encourage spiritual growth throughout the cosmos.

With planets which have taken a rebellious and wayward path, this means quarantine and constant observation, and, where necessary, intervention. This is much like a parent watching a toddler who has just learnt to walk, without the child actually noticing. In order to encourage the child's independence and its natural curiosity, the parent will hold back, refraining from intervening unless there is real danger. If a child happily walks towards fire, the parent will grab its arm before it arrives.

This is what you are collectively doing, citizens of earth: you are WALKING TOWARDS THE FIRE, and it is time to show our faces, move into your field of vision and to hold your hand. And you will hold onto that hand "for dear life" because you will suddenly realise the extremely destructive nature of what you are walking towards.

This is an extreme situation, and we will guide you, yet the goal remains, further along your journey, to make you completely independent and completely SOVEREIGN, completely secure in the knowledge of your own ability to spread love and "light" far and wide, completely confident in your role as a divine being of immense stature, capable of "great things" if you submit to the rules of the cosmos which are intended to increase love and joy at every step for every being in existence.

What can we say to encourage you more, Beloveds, but to say that you will experience the greatest of joy acting as an agent of the DIVINE. We hope that we have been able to clarify for you the extent of your potential, even if you are presently still limited inside a prison of your own collective making. We love you,

Seraphin

Seraphin Message 468: THE FLAG IS FLYING

Through Rosie, 7th November 2021

Dearest Citizens of Earth;
Your day is coming, meaning YOUR DAY OF CHOICE,
WHETHER TO MOVE UPWARDS AND ONWARDS,
irrespective of what it takes, and irrespective of what trauma
surrounds and envelops you, in short WHETHER TO FLY,
or whether you choose to procrastinate, succumb to sadness,
drift aimlessly or "rest on your laurels",
which is the same as refusing to put effort into the WHOLE,
preferring to focus your effort on YOURSELF.
This is the opposite of flying; THIS IS DYING.

THE TIME FOR SELFISHNESS HAS PASSED.
In future, there will only be room for those who consider others,
until the WHOLE WORLD RUNS ON ALTRUISM.

What is the world presently running on, Beloveds? It is most def-
initely MONEY, supported by all the powerful moneyed entities
(by which we mean corporations and organisations as well as
individuals) which uphold the present financial structure and
which ensure your slavery.

This is unheard of on worlds where the level of spirituality is so
much higher than yours. On such worlds, a coarse word or a
veiled insult or any small transgression or misalignment with cosmic law is instantly crushed. If you are about to throw an insult,
you will suddenly become speechless. If you are about to raise a
hand against someone, you will suddenly become paralysed so
that you cannot continue.

Can you imagine the atmosphere on such worlds which are saturated in loving kindness? It means that fear evaporates immediately. It actually means that fear does not exist. Yet on your

kindergarten world, your minds and thus your actions are still clouded by a mixture of propaganda, religious dogma, and the curtains of separation, all of which are propelled by puppeteers in the shadows.

As we have already mentioned, a game is in play, the difference being that in most games, no-one can be sure who the winner is until the very end.

This game however, is under DIVINE CONTROL. For the moment, it may seem that the players can do whatever they like, but the clock is ticking and will put a sudden stop to all proceedings, and this is the moment when your own level of spirituality will be measured, and when you will be sorted accordingly.

Some of you are very caught up in the game. You think it is real. Each day you devour the "new" information which is set before you, assessing it from rigid viewpoints.

YOU ARE BEING PLAYED.

You are not playing in your own right, nor as a result of your own integrity. YET YOU THINK YOU ARE, BECAUSE THE PLAYING FIELD YOU SEE IS FORMED ACCORDING TO YOUR OWN LIMITED IMAGINATION AND KNOWLEDGE.

In actual fact, the playing field is huge (we could also say galactic, universal, eternal and infinite, as an alternative to "huge"), populated by as yet unseen on and off-planet dignitaries and representatives of the administration of the universes.

The time will come when you realise that these persons have been there ALL THE TIME, and that there were actually signs of this. If you had looked upwards, you might have seen THE CELESTIAL FLAG FLYING, SIGNIFYING THE PRESENCE OF THE DIVINE, AND INDICATING THAT "GOD" IS AT HOME, just as flags flying at palaces or embassies might signify the presence of their residents.

All this is preparation: the flag is merely a symbol. What is planned for this earth – and for all those remaining with her – is a sudden shock which will garner ALL OF YOUR ATTENTION and which will mark the actual arrival of divine energy which will penetrate every cell.

This includes your bodies, and as we mentioned, preparation in the form of small "homeopathic" doses has been carried out for some time now, in order to get your bodies "up to speed".

This has of course failed to uplift the majority.

On the contrary: it has led to major health problems resulting from non-physical sources, namely the misalignment with cosmic law, misalignment with high moral principles, and misalignment with the sort of behaviour demonstrated by your most sincere and most revered prophets.

To those who are wearily continuing
without much hope for the future, we advise you to

LOOK UP AT THE FLAG,
FOR IT IS FLYING
DESPITE EVERYTHING "NEGATIVE"
WHICH GREETS YOU.

We wish you courage on the next stage of this journey.

Seraphin

Seraphin Message 469: MOVING TOWARDS FREEDOM

Through Rosie, 20th November 2021

It is only in confinement that you will start to realise the true meaning of FREEDOM. Freedom is a word which has been bandied about at will. It has been used - and its meaning has been corrupted - by its usage in FREEDOM MOVEMENTS, which have been more focused on one particular direction THAN THE WELL-BEING OF THE ONE.

Freedom means FREEDOM FOR EVERYONE, not just the elites, not just those who toe the party line, not just those who lose their inhibitions and revolt against all authority. True freedom is when you are surrounded by people who give freely, love unconditionally and put every effort into uplifting society.

Would it not be wonderful to be on the "receiving end" of this, Citizens of Earth? But to be on the receiving end, and to be included in this scenario, YOU MUST ACT ACCORDINGLY. To scream that you do not want to conform to what everyone else is doing is a childish and selfish response, and a refusal to take on responsibility. The pre-requisite is, of course, that the universal direction taken is a godly one.

Many of you are actually being coerced at this time by this very strategy. You are being told that you must comply with vaccinations and other measures in order to safeguard the health of all.

YET THIS IS NOT GODLY: IT IS BASED ON A LIE.

For those with eyes to see, your roads are not cluttered with fleets of ambulances rushing to assist the afflicted. Neither are people falling down dead in the streets on all sides. Neither do your statistics meet the criteria of truth. They have been manipulated or are presented in a way which leaves out a large portion of what is actually happening.

Freedom is knowing that everyone you encounter is going to treat you in an honest and kind way. It is time to BE that honesty and kindness, irrespective of vaccination status or of any other METHOD OF SEPARATION which has been systematically and deliberately introduced by your governments, banks, pharmaceutical industries and industrial magnates in order to control and gain increasing power.

When will you wake up, Beloveds?
Will you be able to reframe your convictions and beliefs?
Will you realise that even before this supposed pandemic, you were not living in a truly free society?

There have already been so many SCAMDEMICS of all description which have surreptitiously blinded you without you noticing, and this has been going on for millennia – a perspective which also fails to reach you because your historical records present the past in a way which is not favourable to you, and which cements your prisons.

If you are able to hold out in this very difficult period, self-reflecting daily and keeping a sharp eye on the "holes in the narrative", then you will "wise up" to the dreadful mess and the harrowing actions which have been perpetrated without your knowledge and without your conscious approval.

If you can cope with looking all this head on, and if you can rise to the occasion, you have the calibre to change the situation in the future. You will be the pioneers of the future. You will have seen atrocities develop, during which you yourself acted in such a naïve and "sheep like" manner. The poignancy of this experience will never leave you. It will fuel your mission eternally to prevent such reoccurring, and to create the opposite.

We have touched on these topics before, warning you that there is a very heavy legacy which you will have to bear, individually and collectively, yet now it is beginning to dawn on some of you what we really mean. This is not for the compliant or for the faint-hearted: the degree of depravity runs so deep that one glimpse of same will send the faint-hearted into cardiac arrest or instant paralysis. We warn those who are strong that you will have to deal with those who are not. And as always, compassion is a major consideration.

To be grieved by terrible crimes is completely understandable, especially to the degree that you have created on earth, and so compassion must be the first response. Yet the second response is to encourage action. This means being able to offer sympathy but also being able to help people "snap out of it" and undertake essential work.

With this we hope to have helped you better understand your personal roles in the coming times. No one would wish such intensity upon you, dear ones, yet you have brought it upon yourselves, and while we will be helping, there is no one but yourselves who can correct this situation long-term.

Our hearts ache for you.
We do not rejoice in using strong language.
We would rather shower you with love.

May you go firmly forward and solid in your conviction
that what you are doing is extremely important
for the continuation of humankind on this planet.

Seraphin

Seraphin Message 470: A THOUSAND FACES OF YOU

Through Rosie, 27th November 2021

Can you remember, Beloveds, when you lost something precious? Perhaps it was a rucksack or handbag which contained all your most important papers, keys and money? Can you remember the feeling of absolute dread and desperation because you can now no longer go where you want to go, buy what you want to buy, or unlock what you want to unlock? But the most acute sense of loss might be aroused by losing your passport and your supposed identity.

Who are you, if undefined?
Who are you, without possessions?
Who are you without a birthday or parents
Who are you without a country assigned to your name?

Suffice to say that such a situation – or an even worse situation where your home may be destroyed or burnt to the ground – is preparation for what you call DEATH, for as you know, nothing and no one can accompany you through that door. Yet it is a door which leads to a new room and old friends, and you take your learning experiences with you to start a new journey which is determined by yourself in conjunction with celestial advisors.

You will slip into another body. You will take on a new face. And yes, some of you have already done this 1000 times and more. We choose the number 1000 because it is a number you can grasp. Yet life is unlimited, if chosen, providing that your motivation is to help others and to stay within the bounds of cosmic law.

One of those laws, which must be recognized, is the LAW OF ONE. This does not only mean that we should all develop solidarity with each other, as members of the same cosmic family. It also means that every facet of ourselves, our every thought and action, goes into a huge melting pot which combines the thoughts and actions of all. This pot is continually on the boil, processing everything which goes into it continuously, and in accordance with the "ingredients" it is fed with, it will present a delicious and well-balanced soup, or a putrid mess.

This is another way of saying that you are incredibly important, EACH ONE OF YOU, and that your influence is manifold. You add your own unique taste to the pot, and it is never "lost", even if you live like a hermit. You can see yourself, as well as others, in the "end product". When you look into the pot you see yourself as "identical" to others, on the same level, with the same learning abilities, the same responsibilities and the same potential.

When you look into the pot, you see 1000 FACES OF YOU.

If we apply this metaphor to your world, everyone you meet is a reflection of you and part of you. If you have truly understood this, there will be zero tolerance for any designations which are de-signed to separate you. It will be as if you have all lost your birth-day, your parentage, your passport, your status, your positions of importance, your appearance. In short, you will greet each other as loving individuals of an extremely large family. You will see no more differences. You will not be distracted by any shows of wealth or symbols of superiority. You will instantly have 1000 devoted friends.

As we said before, the number 1000 is merely symbolic. We can easily extend this to 9 billion friends – the present number of in-habitants on your planet. And, if you can take it, we can easily extend this number to countless trillions, for that is the number of beings inhabiting what you call OUTER SPACE. We would like to remind you that outer space is actually INNER SPACE in the sense that it is all part of the huge cosmic "pot", and the song you sing will be part of the great cosmic song.

We hope to have broadened your perspectives with this message, for we see that your tiny lives so often centre on issues which would instantly lose their significance if you considered them from the perspective of the GREATER WHOLE. May these thoughts be an inspiration to you going forward, in anticipation of reconnecting to your cosmic brothers and sisters, an event which approaches and which will in time manifest. Know that they will also be part of the cosmic family, and part of you.

What sort of welcome will you give them, Beloveds?

Let me remind you that they are "long lost friends", and that it is earth's inhabitants who long ago decided to cut off their connections to the Divine Family.

May the reunion be smooth and joyous. Seraphin

Seraphin Message 471: A DIVINE MANIFOLD BEING

Through Rosie, 29th November 2021

Many of you earth inhabitants today are convinced of your insignificance and mediocrity, struggling to jump myriad, unpleasant hurdles, only to sink into a chair at the end of the day completely exhausted. Your thoughts circle purely around your daily routine, what you are going to eat, how you can get the chores done, how you can support your families, and a host of other necessities (or non-necessities like "entertainment") forced upon you, which keep you fully occupied. Thinking – which is as much as developing the mind or growing spiritually - is pushed to the back of your minds, if you think at all.

And thus, you are missing out on the main purpose of life, which is to grow, expand, and assist others to do the same. Parents will be well aware of this responsibility, for they see their children developing - or not – according to the time and attention given to them. Time, or lack of it, is a major consideration on your twisted world, and you can be sure that there are many negative forces at work ensuring that you have NO TIME AT ALL. For this would mean major reflection and major change, which is not in their interest, though it would surely be in your own interest.

And it is because you are so "stuck" in routine, so stuck in clamouring onto this and that, so fearful to change anything, that an immense flow of energy is being introduced to your planet which will sweep you away. You can imagine yourself swimming in a river when a huge rush of water suddenly comes downhill. There is no way of avoiding it. You can hold onto a rock for dear life. And you can try to climb out of the river to avoid it completely. You have the choice. Or you can let go of everything and flow with it, open to all new possibilities and opportunities, seeing where it will take you.

Will you go with this flow, Beloveds, or will you watch passively on the river banks, wondering where you could have gone? Will you exhaust yourselves, holding onto the rocks while the heavy weight of water crushes you increasingly with every breath?

You can also compare experiencing this wave of energy to being caught in stormy high winds and rain. Everything which is not tied down, or in this case, which is not anchored in truth, will fly away. All flimsy, poorly-built structures will be destroyed. At the same time, the rain will nourish the waiting seeds. And at this juncture, you must ask yourselves if you are the waiting seeds, and whether you have "great projects" to germinate.

We can call this a "cosmic wave", for it does not originate on your planet. Its job is to kick you into motion and to encourage you to leave everything which is pointless, stale, low quality, corrupt and stagnant BEHIND. It will penetrate every pore. It will search out that which is blocked and damaged. It will destroy that which is no longer capable of sustaining life. It will build up that which is uplifting. It will repair that which has potential. It will raise your consciousness, if you are capable of self-reflection. It will "dumb you down" if you offer resistance to spiritual growth.

Is it becoming clear what is happening here, Beloveds? There is no escape. You may choose, of course, to remain in your humdrum lives, repeating your daily routine like a broken record, but this will lead you nowhere, at least, to nowhere on this planet, for this wave will continue to flood everything, and if you cannot align yourself with it, you must go elsewhere.

You may feel, in the face of these words, like a small ant which is trying to climb an enormous mountain. We say that even a small ant is capable of great feats, and that every effort in the right direction (by which we mean in alignment with cosmic law) will be supported. Do not lose heart, but strive to "do good" and strive to learn. The wave will assist you. If, on the other hand, you wish to disregard information such as that we are trying to tell you, and if you think you are impervious to any incoming wave, completely convinced that you are untouchable, it is your choice to believe this, in the sense of exercising your free will, but you will be subjected nevertheless because the wave is here BY DIVINE DECREE, MARKING THE END OF AN AGE.

You are welcome to move on into the new age on planet earth, or to leave. Why would you be given that choice, Beloveds? Because you create your own lives. You determine where you will go next. Your existence and your essence is not necessarily limited to one life, one incarnation, or one planet.

Many of you are not ants but
BEINGS OF IMMENSE STATURE.

If we were to ask the question WHO ARE YOU, it would be appropriate to answer I AM A DIVINE MANIFOLD BEING.

We know that these words may sound overdone to you, but this is because you have not fully entertained the thought of your great potential. Neither has it dawned upon you that you are incredibly important for the next stage of events. Otherwise, why would you be here? We would like to encourage you to augment your view of yourselves to fit DIVINE SHOES, making a DIVINE CONTRIBUTION, and we encourage you to elevate your behaviour accordingly, for your earth sorely needs you. Seraphin.

Seraphin Message 472: FRAGILITY

Through Rosie, 15th December 2021

It is in your most extreme moments of fragility, inhabitants of earth, that you will have access to the greatest insights. You are presently experiencing many situations, restrictions and absurdities which are unsettling you and biting you to the bone, even affecting the "bone marrow", the very heart of you.

How do you react if your world suddenly turns upside-down? Do you turn upside down with it, or do you return to your original position, while regarding everything else go "haywire"? You will note that we are using lots of current expressions here to try and get the present feeling of tension across. Those among you who are extremely sensitive, or who have very high goals and who are frustrated at the lack of movement forward, will be particularly affected and may reach the point of despair, with a wish to end it all now.

This is how suicides occur – due to a feeling of absolute hope-lessness that nothing can improve. Yet this is a very intense feel-ing AT ONE PARTICULAR MOMENT, and it includes the convic-tion that you CAN see into the future, and that you know that the future holds not one iota of light which you can latch onto. You are convinced that you are caught in a timeless and bottomless pit, for all eternity, and that nothing will ever change.

This - to put not too fine a point upon it - is extremely short-sighted. We can assure you that this is not so. How can you, with limited knowledge in a world of lies, attempting to swim and keep your head above water, possibly have an accurate view of what is really going on? Do you want to know what is really going on? If so, you will pull yourself out of the river, stand on the banks and watch from the shore. You might even look up at the sky, for there you may find infinite inspiration - spots of light which are actually huge universes.

We would ask you, in your fragility, to search out the points of light, knowing that they contain a wealth of experience which you cannot yet possibly imagine. Spend an hour, or even a few minutes, watching the sky and the stars, and you will enter a whole new dimension of thinking. You will be transferred to a dif-ferent level. You will experience calm. You will get a sense of what eternity really means, and you will realise that this is just a "traffic jam" on a very small planet.

However, small or not, it is significant. We are not advocating here that you say to yourselves "well, in that case, nothing really matters". We are advising you to step back and yield to the greater visions of things which we, your galactic brothers and sis-ters, are carrying for you and which will come into view in the future.

Meanwhile we ask you to RECOGNISE THAT YOU ARE IN A FRAGILE STATE and to discontinue that which would push you "over the edge", since highly sensitive and responsible souls are sorely needed for the era which succeeds this one.

If you are not in a stable mental state, seek ways of "stepping out of the fray" and avoiding the "madding crowd". Look to your way of life, your health, your family and your associates. Do not get embroiled in a thousand discussions which are mostly speculation and directed by fear. Listen within and follow your inner voice, rather than being distracted by those who are worried, needy and oppressive.

Again, this does not mean develop selfishness: it means acting compassionately when the situation requires it, but do not rush to take on all burdens. Firstly, you will not be able to do this, because the present burdens are so heavy and so many. Secondly, problems can only be solved by those who carry them. One may offer help, yes, but personal responsibility for finding the solution must be given to the carrier.

You may feel that this is a "make or break" situation – that it may be the end of the world. It is the end of the world as you know it, and for this to happen, and for wonders to ensue, you must let go. This is part of the process. Total collapse is also part of the process. Do not sink into oblivion when you see this collapse coming, and crawl screaming into your hideouts, but welcome it with open arms, knowing that at last, there is a wonderful chance for people to come to their senses, and for society to renew itself FROM SCRATCH. Use the time to brainstorm with your family and colleagues. What would you change if you could, because the circumstances will be given in which everything is possible. We would gently draw you back from the abyss, dear ones, from the brink of self-destruction, so that you retire for a while to envisage a world without precipices.

We hope that we could provide you with some inspiration with this message, which is intended for all those who are suffering at this time. Remember that the new dawn will break, and that the light of day inevitably follows the dark night. Seraphin

Seraphin Message 473: ALL ENDS ARE BEGINNINGS

Through Rosie, 26th December 2021

Can you think back, Beloveds, to a time when you were in severe shock due to an unexpected event? This may have been the sudden end of a relationship which you thought was stable, or the sudden death of a person you thought was healthy and would live forever.

Nothing lasts forever, my friends, if your view is limited to this one life. Yet "forever" is certainly possible, and indeed the norm, if you consider "reincarnation" and multiple lives. For those of you who continuously strive to perfect yourselves and try to attain Christ consciousness, eternity is a certainty.

Nothing is as permanent as change – as it is often sadly stated on your distraught world, for the changes experienced are usually unpleasant, yet change should be welcomed with open arms because it signifies the bursting of a festering wound, the explosion of a destructive situation for all to see, the collapse of a flimsy and dangerous "house of cards".

To keep any of these situations intact is not in your interest. It is in your interest to let everything fall, to demolish instable buildings, to expose harmful behaviours which destroy your society, and to expose the propaganda which destroys your minds, turning you into heartless, manipulated beings with no moral conscience or strength. It is easy to rule over people who are depressed, fearful, vulnerable, aggressive and easily triggered so that they harm and accuse each other.

This structure is firmly cemented into your society at present: you have strong (and deliberately promoted) ideas of right and wrong, and those who do not fit into a certain category are ostracized. Those who do not play the game are excluded, belittled and forced to bend to pressures which make them less belligerent to the present overriding narrative.

YET THIS IS ONLY A NARRATIVE,
ENFORCED TO FURTHER YOUR SLAVERY.
AND LIKE ALL FAULTY BUILDINGS
WHICH ARE FOUNDED ON LIES,
AND WHOSE STRUCTURE APPEARS TO BE STABLE
BUT IS ACTUALLY EXTREMELY FLIMSY,
THEY WILL EVENTUALLY FALL.

And the resulting shock will be great and sudden. Many will realise that they simply believed everything they were told by the media, by "experts", by politicians, and by "influencers" in all categories and walks of life.

Also, those who prided themselves on seeing through the narrative and who condemned others for lack of critical thinking, will also realise that they have been "had", that they have been conveniently provided with "critical material" and that their perusal of such was allowed and deliberately encouraged, so that they did not focus on the real framework of all this, which is the eternal cosmic framework. Their minds have been guided towards stories which – although they might counter the official narrative – have been purposely placed in front of their noses to make them think that they are a critical thinker or a "freedom fighter", when actually this is just another method of control.

SO WHAT AND WHERE IS THE TRUTH, you may ask.

Truth – and only a portion of it – is known to the few. They have been attacked and persecuted for their knowledge for millennia. They are not in the public eye. They are not allowed to travel the world giving lectures. If they do actually speak in public, the truth they will utter will always be "partial", so as to avoid repercussions. Some do not hold back, speaking their truth, and some are killed as a result.

However, the "cosmic perspective" also includes cosmic protection for a number of persons, in the form of unseen entities who arrange for safety. They also provide information telepathically which will benefit the listener.

Can you hear, Beloveds?
Will you open yourselves to such realms?
Are you ensconced in the purely material world
or are you susceptible to the Divine inner stirrings
which nudge you forward on a different and more fulfilling path
which is in alignment with your true vocation?

Do you feel a sense of tension, a sense of being caught up in a bottleneck? Are you seized by a feeling of horror when you realise that the world as you know it is incredibly fragile and that it could break any second? Are you aware that irreparable change is coming, and that a huge END is looming on the horizon?

Some of you will shake your heads when you read this, crying that much has been prophesied and that nothing has happened. Yet this is gross deception and demonstrates arrogance. How can one person possibly understand what is happening on a global scale, being familiar with every network, every development and every detail? If you feel deep disappointment, it is because you have given up hope. Yet the END is still looming on the horizon, irrespective of whether you lift your eyes towards it, glowing with joy and anticipation, or whether you turn towards the darkness in deep resignation.

Let us return to our original question: do you remember the feeling of utter disbelief, shock and sorrow when a beloved friend departs or "dies"? Imagine this feeling a thousand-fold, for it will not just be the disappearance of one dear friend: for many, in addition, it will be the death of their convictions, their religions, their purpose in life, their views of the world and how life should be lived. It will be the collapse of their comfortable way of life.

What follows will be an intense period of readjustment, of releasing the old and of accepting that you really had no idea at all about the real depth of depravity, about the real cost of human life, about the real pyramids of power, about the interconnectedness of a huge and all-inclusive grid of evil, about the exclusion of this planet from its galactic neighbours due to extreme "bad behaviour" and due to the danger of contamination, resulting in quarantine.

Only the humble and far-sighted among you will be able to complete such a "turnaround". It will demand extreme soul-searching and "mental gymnastics".

There will be many tears,
many "cleaning up" operations and
many re-orientation sessions as you struggle to discover
WHERE YOU COLLECTIVELY WENT WRONG.

This will be a very painful process, but when you have ultimately understood, you will voluntarily uphold very strict measures to ensure that this will not happen again. Your world will turn into a galactic study centre for rebellious worlds – a museum to show others the devastating consequences of deviating from the DIVINE PATH, as well as demonstrating the ideal community and behaviour which is manifested by a RETURN TO THE DIVINE

PLAN, producing a world which hosts the perfect ambiance for spiritual growth, and the perfect place for the next generation to grow into fulfilled, positive and responsible individuals.

Is this a dream, Beloveds?

No. It is your next reality when the END shows its face, indicating the start of wonderful NEW BEGINNINGS. With this thought we leave you, Seraphin.

Seraphin Message 474: CONTROLLED DEMOLITION

Through Rosie, 2nd January 2022

Dear Inhabitants of Earth: it has come to this; the "dark side", which has been in control of your enslavement for millennia, is now being "taken out". The more cynical among you will say:

NO. I CANNOT SEE ANY SIGN OF THIS.
I CAN ONLY SEE THE ESTABLISHMENT
OF WORLD DICTATORSHIP.
I CAN ONLY SEE PEOPLE WHO SUCCUMB TO POWER.

Yet the fact that you, at this moment, cannot "see"
is not an indication of reality, or of the real situation "at large".
It is your limited perspective only.

Do you think, Beloveds, that we will deliver a fanfare, round up all the culprits at once and televise their hangings simultaneously around the world? This is not only not feasible, but also extremely unwise. It is not possible to take short cuts (especially short cuts to knowledge and wisdom) or to endanger others just to satisfy your penchant for the spectacular or to pander to your ideas of sudden and immediate retribution, or to end your impatience.

Imagine you are responsible for taking down a large office building. Would you simply drop a bomb on it as soon as possible? Or would you first remove anything of value, examining the contents carefully? Would you sift through important papers, or valuable equipment, or records of transactions, or accounts of personnel? Would you not examine all corners, including those which have all but escaped your memory, just in case something important gets destroyed? Would you inspect everything before giving orders to bring down the building? Would you consider the surrounding buildings, and how they might be affected by the blast? And wouldn't you arrange for experts to assess the structure of the building, and how and where it might fall, in the case of controlled demolition?

And would you warn nearby residents that something momentous is going to happen (and these messages fit into this category), and would you not find the very best moment to carry the demolition out, taking manpower and the weather into account? And would you not arrange for the fire brigade and other emergency services to be on hand, just on case something goes wrong?

And when the demolition is over, would you not have arranged for teams of workers to remove the rubble and clear the ground? And when "tabula rasa" has been achieved, would you not already have your new plans in hand, ready to manifest a new dream for this piece of land? Would you not have made designs for this new space which has opened up?

Do you think that the celestial representatives in charge of this operation would simply "drop a bomb", or do you think that they would plan meticulously, carrying out their mission with compassion and excellence, completing their task with great attention to detail? Do you think that the celestials would simply "give up" or "give in" or "hope for the best" or succumb to impatience, just trying to end this thing as soon as possible?

You will learn that this period of "winding down" has been very, very long, and that it has involved multiple preparations on multiple levels. The celestials are also aware of the multiple repercussions of this on 9 billion people, and sufficient provision has been made for everyone one of them. We are trying here to introduce you not only to the complexity of your situation but also to the very complex "unravelling" which has needed to take place before this planet can move forward to its true destiny.

You will note our use of the past tense – "has needed". We are close to the "FINISHING LINE". But as you will discover, this does not mean that all is well, or that an end has somehow been reached, after which you can conveniently have a rest or heave a sigh of relief. No: this is the beginning of so many revelations which will take your breath away.

Will you still be able to function, Beloveds? Will you be able to overcome your shock and step into action like the true spiritual warriors you would like to be? Will you be so overcome by emotion that you are incapable of helping others? Will you relish the fact that you were right all along, and will this pride prevent your compassion? Will you try and help others understand, despite the fact that they treated you so badly and misunderstood you so thoroughly in the past?

This message consists mainly of questions for you, the protagonists, to contemplate before the "shit hits the fan" in an obvious manner. This is actually a very mild description of what you will be faced with. Call on your inner guide, the voice of divine intuition, whenever you are in need, for those around you may be incapable of making decisions and of looking after themselves. When they are suffering paralysis, you must be capable of going into action. When they are sad, you must be capable of taking them into your arms and of offering words of encouragement. When they are desperate, you must be able to give them hope, and when they are distraught, you must be able to comfort them, showing compassion but also encouraging them to partake in co-creating a new and better future.

This may sound like a "pep talk". It is indeed. We see the need to prepare you ones mentally so that you can be of optimal service to your fellow humans. Seraphin

Seraphin Message 475:
ELITES, EXILE AND FRAGILE FACADES

Through Rosie, 8TH JANUARY 2022

Listen to us please, Beloveds. We are sending you yet another message, though this scribe is not really in the mood for it just now, and we understand that many of you are tired of this really DISGRACEFUL scenario in which so many have "FALLEN FROM GRACE", resulting in an extremely depraved and also dangerous situation on a global scale.

This may be difficult for you to believe if you are very concentrated on your own routines and your present tasks. Yet the perspective of what living as a human being really means, and your real purpose here, will shatter your present concepts.

We would like to discuss three phenomena here.
The first is ELITES.

Your "elites", who have for so long held all power in their hands, have SELF-ELECTED THEMSELVES. They are self-appointed controllers and families who have given all their loyalty to one source, and that source is ungodlike, acting ferociously and without any compassion whatsoever in order to wield optimal power. That you cannot see it, or that it pervades and controls every aspect of what you consider your life to be, has no bearing on the fact that it exists. This situation has occurred because you, the "victims" in this scenario, have not considered yourself "elite": you consider yourselves small, ineffective, struggling to find a foothold, fighting to get by. You do not see yourselves as sovereign, equal in weight to all other sovereigns, choosing to make your own rules. Of course, this can easily go astray if your rules are not in alignment with celestial law, but if they are, there is no limit to your standing, your success and also your joy. Thus each individual must become an "elite", not in the sense of wielding power or gathering riches, but in the sense of becoming a true and valued member of society with a mind of your own, and whose intentions are only good.

The second concept we wish to draw your attention to is EXILE.

In exile, where you are cut off from your roots and normal surroundings, you will encounter tremendous hardships, but you will also have the chance to develop incredible bravery and you will be forced to stand your ground and develop your character. This is what you are doing here on earth, Beloveds. You are in exile. You are cut off from your divine roots, from your heritage as representatives of cosmic law, as manifestors of divine will.

Is this really my job description, you may ask? Indeed, it is so, and the fact that you cannot remember or do not realise it shows that your period of learning in exile could have been more profitably spent. You are cut off from your galactic brothers and sisters, indeed you may be completely unaware of them, or they may enter your minds like a vague but unreal memory.

Others, however, have sought telepathic communication, for thoughts traverse the universe, irrespective of boundaries set up by celestial administration, such as the limits imposed on this rebellion world which you call earth. Many of you consider earth your home, whereas it is in fact just a station you are passing through. When your minds are more open, you will laugh at yourselves, because there is actually no exile anywhere. The whole universe is your home. This you will see, if you adhere to cosmic law, if you make helping others your task, and when you see the whole situation from the point of view of eternity.,

The third concept we would like to discuss is
FRAGILE FACADES.

We are at the stage when the illusion of separation – despite all strategies employed by the "elite" – is about to crumble. Many facades have been established for your supposed "protection", and being of a fearful nature, you have swallowed up these stories and accepted these convenient offers with open arms. Yet such facades are extremely thin and are starting to crack. What may have seemed to be "rock solid" is actually only a piece of ice which is melting under the heat of the sun. What looks like a dead end is actually a completely new beginning. What looks like total tyranny is actually just a last attempt to hold on to power. What looks like dire warnings and stipulations in media outlets, fanning fear in all directions, is in fact the last desperate attempt of a controlling media to retain that control.

Yet all this will crumble, and you will be shocked to find the rubble at your feet. This will be a test of your flexibility, or your ability to stand up in the face of what appears to be tragedy, but which is actually the collapse of tyranny.

Rejoice, for the time approaches. Seraphin

Seraphin Message 476:
PICKING UP PIECES AND LEAVING A TRAIL OF PURITY

Through Rosie, 9th January 2022

As more and more structures, familiar concepts and normal routines start to crumble, dear Inhabitants of Earth, you will see that they all had foundations of sand; that is to say, they were instable, failing in quality, lacking in integrity and incapable of withstanding the truth. They are also irreparable.

What will you do as you see these great "empires" collapsing – empires on which you have relied, empires which have held your lives together, empires which have dominated your thinking and your way of life, empires which have inspired you to reach for certain goals?

All at once, you will realise that these goals were not worth reaching, and that you were actually being steered towards useless and worthless ends, steered away from courses of action which would – if you had put a lot of effort into it – have changed the direction of life on this planet for the better.

Yet you have been grossly deceived. You have played along with the game, and the consequences of all this will now be placed in no uncertain terms in front of your opened eyes.

As you look behind you, you will see a trail of destruction, a shattering of lost dreams, many webs of intrigue and subterfuge on a level which it will be difficult for you to comprehend. You have the choice to turn away in complete denial, or to look back at all the pieces, seeing how they fitted together, and tracing the whole sorry story of how they once formed a construct which took you in completely. As we have said before, you have "been had".

The next question is: what sort of trail do you want to leave behind you now? Is it going to be a flimsy, dodgy set of parameters which allows others to avoid responsibility, which allows them to slip through convenient loopholes, which encourages laziness or a victim mentality? Or will it be a path of purity, of integrity, of honesty, of dedication?

Such a path would build a magnificent "building", brilliant in its architecture, beautiful in its aesthetics, constituting a source of inspiration throughout the universe. It is up to you, citizens of the wayward planet, to construct this cathedral of strength and morality which can never be destroyed, inspiring generations to come, representing the very opposite of the rubble you now see behind you, resulting from your collective actions to date.

Your every thought and deed contributes to the path of purity, if you make the decision to do so. This is your future, if you are prepared to dedicate yourself to it. We hope that we have empowered you with this message, making you aware of your incredible potential, as an individual and therefore also as a collective, in the sense of ALL IS ONE. Seraphin

Seraphin Message 477:
YOUR CHOICE: MIND FOGGING OR MIND JOGGING

Through Rosie, 15th January 2022

Today we would like to tell you in no uncertain terms that the choice of each individual between mind fogging and mind jogging will determine the destiny of your planet, for better or for worse. So serious is the prevalence of "mind fog" that nothing can be seen in complete clarity. It pervades every crevice, every chink in the wall, conveniently filling in every crack in the narrative and every missing link in the chain, leaving you numbed, deceived, imprisoned, bound to debilitating routines and caught within narrow thought constructs.

Trying to clear the fog is a never-ending and very disturbing process since it pours in from all sides continuously, in the form of propaganda, in the form of corrupted "news stories", in the form of glossed over secrets and in the form of multiple measures of distraction which blunt the edge of your critical thinking and which ultimately poison your mind.

Many of you may consider that it is actually your bodies which are most at risk – in view of substandard foods, additives, polluted air and so on, but actually it is the pollution of your MINDS which has led to your demise.

How can one escape fog?

One can try and hide in places which it does not reach, but this keeps you inactive and isolated. If you RECOGNISE THAT THERE IS FOG AT ALL, AND THAT THERE IS SOMETHING MISSING, and IF YOU DO NOT ACCEPT THIS UNIFORM BLANKET OF WHITEWASH AS YOUR ULTIMATE REALITY, YOU MAY BE DRIVEN TO CLIMB A MOUNTAIN AND RISE ABOVE THE "CLOUD" LEVEL.

In this way, you will suddenly gain an overview: you will see everything with piercing clarity (and you will see the overwhelming power and extent of the fog below you). You will be very tired as a result of the steep climb, but the view and the insights it affords will be worth it. You will see great destruction in detail, for the fog will not be strong enough to cover everything once people start climbing the mountain. You will also see great beauty, formerly unseen. And when you descend again into the valley of fog, you will never again see it with the same eyes. You will know that the light exists, even though the sun appears to be concealed.

DO YOU KNOW THAT THE LIGHT ALWAYS EXISTS?
WE MEAN, OF COURSE,
THE LIGHT OF THE DIVINE WHICH OVERSEES ALL.

Some people on your earth call this GOD or LOVE. It is what bestows LIFE. It is what ALLOWS YOU – in the sense of granting you FREE WILL – to create your own experiences – in this case to choose whether to hide, or whether to climb: whether to be passive or active; whether to retreat or whether to jog forwards.

Just like the muscles in your body, the muscles of the mind will deteriorate and will lose strength if not used. Young children are not so much caught in this kind of dilemma. They retain their natural curiosity. They are driven by the desire to learn and grow. But with passing years, the propaganda and mind control which presently reigns on your planet will gradually slow them down into resigned, conforming and complacent individuals.

There is a great need, Beloveds, for you to carry out a "spring cleaning" operation on your minds, dusting out forgotten corners, exercising "muscles" which have gone into disuse or even dystrophy, promoting critical thinking and generally questioning everything which you have taken for granted.

It is also time to JOG YOUR MEMORY.

This can be seen on two levels: firstly, remember the glimpses of pure happiness and content which you have experienced. Push away the heavy blanket of fog which has obscured them from your memory for so long. Consider how to regenerate such exquisite moments of pure peace, and creatively go into action to reconstruct same.

The second level is much more significant. We ask you to jog your memory of WHO YOU REALLY ARE. This is not restricted to your present identity in your present body in your present life.

Your "soul" or "essence" or "personality" has existed before this life, and it will continue beyond this one, on a constant quest to learn, improve and to use this knowledge to help others. Exceptions are those who are part "robotoid" and who demonstrate "machine mind", for they cannot conceive of learning, or of personal progress, or of expanding their own journey to include the journeys of ALL, in the sense of feeling compassion for or connection to the global or even the cosmic community.

You will see that we address some huge perspectives here. We are trying to bring you out of the fog and to push you up the mountain so that you can clearly see which path to take next. We love you and would guide you the best we can, Seraphin.

Seraphin Message 478: THE MYRIAD PARTICLES OF YOU

Through Rosie, 15th January 2022

Have you ever wondered, Inhabitants of Earth, how many hair follicles there are in your skin? Or have you wondered how many hairs are on your head? Or have you wondered how many species of wildlife your earth has ever supported (and unfortunately how many species you have exterminated)?

And have you ever imagined how long it might take to count all the stars in the cosmos, or to document their individual histories for eternity? Can you imagine that there are beings who have been entrusted with this very task? Can it be that the history of your earth is also minutely documented, right from the very beginning, noting the first stirrings of life, the emergence of developing mind, and the many strivings and failings to set up lasting moral civilizations?

To ask these questions is to attempt to extend your horizons beyond the restrictive limitations you have encountered. These limitations have been partly imposed by others who are responsible for this part of the cosmos. In their capacity as administrators, protectors and officers who ensure order, they have instructed earth to remain in quarantine so that she (or rather her violent and destructive inhabitants) do not contaminate their planetary neighbours.

Yet another barrage of restrictions has been imposed upon you by those you refer to as the "elite", the "cabal" or the "illuminati" or the "deep state". You have so many different names, yet the names do not matter. What does matter is that they all belong to the glove of the same hand, and that the hand belongs to one who is (temporarily) powerful yet nameless.

But by far the greatest set of limitations you live under has been imposed by YOURSELVES due to a lack of development of MIND (which we emphasized in the last message) and a lack of SPIRITUAL LIVING.

You pander to old superstitions, to the powers in control, to the money system, and to many other systems. You fail to question. You follow the dogma. You bow to gurus and you capitulate to your overlords. You chase mammon instead of adhering to solid, honourable values. You treat each other like dross, like stepping stones to achieve power, money or momentary exhilaration.

When will all this stop, Beloveds?

We will not tire of writing about it until it does, and we will assist all who plea to us for help. We are always at your bidding, as are your own personal guides, to bring you further along the spiritual path.

If you have no experience in communication with the unseen, then we entreat you first to contemplate nature in order to enter a state of wonder. Our initial questions in this message will lead you there.

Contemplate also not only the wonders, intricacy and divine blueprints exhibited in the natural world, resulting in the growth of the perfectly proportioned tree or the perfectly proportioned rose, but contemplate also the intricacy of YOURSELF, including all the cells and particles which are arranged perfectly and which communicate constantly and effectively with each other, without requiring you to do anything.

Can you see the UNSEEN at work here?

All this will indicate to you that there is, by divine design and unseen administration, a plan for you. Your perfect functioning is leading you to your purpose. You are occupying a vehicle so that you have a means to execute that specific purpose, just as a flower will bloom and then go forth to produce seeds (and we are not referring to producing offspring here: we are referring to what you have come here to create).

You are, to put it bluntly,
DIVINELY SUPPORTED
IN AN UNSEEN WAY
BY A GREAT POWER.

The representatives and helpers of this great power are your unseen guides who will present you with all sort of helpful opportunities, and who will prevent you from going down disastrous paths, if you will listen. As their name suggests, they are capable of GUIDING YOU IN THE RIGHT DIRECTION. They see your mistakes. They are familiar with your thoughts, with your addictions, with your foregone conclusions and with your weaknesses. They know every particle of you. They are also familiar with all your strengths and all your potential, and it is this which they choose, out of love for you, to support and promote.

We send this message to you to strengthen your sense of purpose, to emphasise the importance of your development in a GODLY manner, and to ensure that you know about the advice and support which is available to you on your journey. Seraphin

Seraphin Message 479:
THE LIGHT AT THE END OF THE TUNNEL

Through Rosie, 21st January 2022

If you look carefully, Beloveds, there will be a tiny spot of light on the horizon, irrespective of any unfortunate situations you may find yourselves in, irrespective of any looming calamity, tragedy or insurmountable corruption which is slowly pushing its ugly head towards the surface for all to see.

Be aware that this light exists, but do not focus on it exclusively, for you are walking along the edge of a mountain - the very apex of a mountain - and the sides are steep, and if you should lose your foothold you will tumble into the abyss, and then the light will certainly no longer be in your view. You must walk with awareness at all times.

Sometimes the tunnel seems so dark and so endless that you feel very depressed and sad, and so you hang your head, thus averting your gaze from the point of light in the distance. You may know in your subconscious that the light exists, but you no longer have any visible proof of it. We ask you to lift your heads and follow the light, taking into consideration all the meanings that the word "light" carries.

We ask you to retain awareness, not only of the light in the distance but also of the light in your immediate surroundings which can be found in very small details. It can be the laugh of a child. It can be a snowflake on your window. It can be a sudden realization that this cannot go on forever. Carry this comforting thought in your hearts, Beloveds, for the times are extremely difficult and are about to increase in difficulty.

YOU YOURSELF ARE THAT LIGHT
AT THE END OF THE TUNNEL

And because you walk along a precarious mountain ridge, you can be seen by those who toil below and who do not have the strength to climb to such a height and who cannot, in fact, see the point of light on the distant horizon.

Thus you are their encouragement, and you are also their connection to the divine light in the distance. It would be too much for them to conceive of this, but they can conceive of you, ever moving forward, ever progressing, ever greeting them with an optimistic view, ever meeting them with a smiling face. You are positioned all over the world at strategic points in order to spread your light, not in order to hang your heads. We beseech you to remember this as the clouds unfold in the coming storm.

Again, we would like to say that
YOU ARE THE LIGHT AT THE END OF THE TUNNEL.

It is not something which is separate from you. YOU ARE THE SUN, and the more you shine, the quicker the ice will melt in the hearts of the people around you, the quicker the rigidity of the structures you have imposed upon yourselves will crumble, and the quicker everyone will progress towards the end of the tunnel where a new world and a new life is awaiting.

Seraphin Message 480:
TERRIBLE SECRETS AND THE RESILIENCE OF YOU

Through Rosie, 29th January 2022

We address you once more in these very difficult times, beloved inhabitants of Earth. Our sadness increases daily as we watch the majority of you fail to actively discern, fail to address the very grave problems on your earth plane, and fail to extend your compassion – if it exists at all – to those you do not know personally. It is time to expand your perspectives on all levels. And because you are not capable of doing this yourselves, except in very few cases, it is necessary for energies from OUTSIDE your planet to expose that which you do not want to see, to provide a very hard but very much required learning lesson, and to point you in a new direction.

This involves the revelation of "terrible secrets", which have actually been in existence for many, many years, even decades or centuries or beyond, and which have so far been successfully repressed by those who wield the power on your planet, in order to retain that power and in order to better control and diminish you. And you are not even aware that you live under this yoke. Your monetary and other systems are considered by you to be completely "normal", whereas they are actually a method of ensuring slavery.

Do you think we are exaggerating, Beloveds? How do you feel every day? Are your little lives permeated with worry, about the next paycheck, about the next bills to pay, about the next virus, about the next war? Is your attention swallowed by the daily struggle, or is your imagination allowed to soar so that you have the mental space and practical amenities to develop into the very best version of yourselves in service to the rest of humanity? Most of you will certainly answer NO.

What is the quality of these secrets, you may ask? They will be revealed, so there is not much point going into details here, but they involve deliberate murder on a massive scale, and obstruction to justice on a massive scale. They involve orchestrated operations to subdue, poison and kill you and to keep you running on the spot like a hamster in a wheel. You think you are running – moving forward at a strong pace – but actually you are at a standstill.

When these revelations occur, how will you react? Will you go into complete denial and turn your heads away? Will you recognize that you have been thoroughly duped? Will you be humble enough to admit that you had a hand in it – if not by deliberate perpetration then through passive compliance? Will you have the resilience to face it all, forgive all and to forgive yourself?

If you encounter difficulties, it may help to take another look at WHAT YOU REALLY ARE. Some of you will say that you are your body. This is a misconception. There will always be THE ESSENCE OF YOU, which we could also call your personality or your soul or that which makes you completely unique. This exists continuously, irrespective of what form you take, or what "temperature" you presently find yourself in. Contemplate the properties of water: it may become hard and frozen, and it may crack when someone walks across it. It may turn into steam in high temperatures, or it may turn into snow at low temperatures. It may expand as ice. It may divide into tiny droplets. It may merge into great seas. But all the time, it is water. The same is true of you: whatever "body" or "form" you may assume, the essence of you remains the same.

In the face of dealing with all the terrible secrets to be revealed, remember at all times that THIS IS JUST TEMPORARY and that YOUR ESSENCE IS ALWAYS THE SAME.

We could also say that your DIVINE ORIGIN is always the same. Or that your ETERNAL JOURNEY always continues, irrespective of your present form.

Many of you – not all – are on the eternal journey, and these new developments on your planet will serve to enlighten you and MOVE YOU ONWARDS ON YOUR SPIRITUAL JOURNEY.

For this, you can ultimately be thankful. For this you can fall on your knees in gratitude. For this, you can feel deep relief that the horrible feeling of "not knowing" and your suspicion that there is something dreadful going on, which has been lurking in your sub-conscious for years, is finally confirmed and exposed. As we have said before, only a hard look at these "secrets" will enable them to be dissipated and corrected. We are in the "correcting time", and you will see that there are so many things which need correcting, that you will all have your hands full.

So be not overburdened by grief. So sink not into oblivion, not bearing to look, but stride forward with courage and go into what-ever positive action you can muster. Thus will you create a better world than the one you have left behind. We know that we have said this sort of thing before, but due to acute present situations, we feel impelled to do so again. Seraphin.

Seraphin Message 481: MEASURING YOUR PROGRESS

Through Rosie, 5ᵗʰ February 2022

Can you imagine, Citizens of Earth, that we of the "celestial realms" beyond your planet are capable of monitoring your every thought, action and intention at any given time, capable of as-sessing your position of the spiritual ladder at any point in the present and past? Can you imagine that the technology used to undertake such "tracking" – on a purely physical level – is being developed on your earth as we speak, using the excuse of rampant disease (and what will be the next excuse, you may wonder) to round you up and suck out all your statistics? Your "likes" and "dislikes" have also been collected in an intensive and intrusive manner by your various social media.

Some of you are wary of all this, such as this scribe who has only given two "likes" in her whole life, in her recollection, but we say that there is nothing problematic about collecting data, or about moving towards this sort of transparency, IF IT IS USED FOR HOLY PROJECTS. And one of these holy projects – the most important - is to FURTHER YOUR SPIRITUAL GROWTH. IT IS THIS SPIRITUAL GROWTH WHICH WILL CHANGE EVERY-THING FOR THE BETTER.

Some of you may have some understanding of what this is all about – the progression from being a perhaps somewhat naïve, egotistical and agitated being to becoming a serene, confident and altruistic "helper". But this, if we look back not only at your progress and experience in this particular life, actually goes much deeper, although you cannot "recall" it. We have access to all records of your previous incarnations and activities, whenever and wherever they were, in the rest of the universe. The circle of people on which you bestow your "helpfulness", and thus YOUR-SELVES, may start out as your original family, but it grows to include whole galaxies.

This is beyond the present scope of your "knowing": the small human brain can only contain and process a certain amount, though it can open up communications with a larger "pool of knowledge" when in a meditative state. We are trying to introduce here THE SIGNIFICANCE OF YOU ON A WIDER SCALE, and to reiterate that you are not simply "helpers" restricted to one life on a small wayward planet.

Your influence never fades.
YOU ARE MANIFESTORS OF THE DIVINE
IN MANY PLACES, FOR ALL TIME.

Many of you have chosen to "manifest the Divine" at this very problematic time on planet earth. It is precisely because of the problematic circumstances which are brewing and destined to explode to dramatic effect that you have stepped up to the challenge of penetrating this thick blanket of darkness with your particular light.

If we, the observers, assess the present "progress potential" of average earth dwellers, we would have no hope at all about steering you away from self-destruction. You who have come to spread "light" are essential to the "turning it all around" process. So do not underestimate yourselves or retire into comfortable corners. Your mission is not to experience comfort but to urge others forward on their spiritual journeys.

There will be many who turn away. There will be many who will have no idea what you are talking about. You must choose your words with wisdom whenever a "window" opens. You should not expend your energy by forcing anyone to listen, if they do not want to do so of their own accord. Do not launch into rants which do nothing but alienate. IF you see opportunities, grasp them 100 percent and grasp them with gratitude. If you find yourself peering into an abyss, it will remain an abyss irrespective of how long you stare down into it, and irrespective of how many times you call "Is there anyone out there?", without getting a reply.

We are measuring you with a spiritual ruler, dear friends, for this is our duty. It is spiritual progress alone which will "save" your planet and steer her towards a safe course and a secure harbour.

Seraphin

Seraphin Message 482: DIVIDE AND FALL

Through Rosie, 10th February 2022

This is the time, Beloveds, of extreme contradictions, and there will never again be such an extreme period in your history as to what you are presently facing. You will find – simultaneously – "peace-loving" nations who are on a war path. You will find heroes and heroines implementing extreme measures to save children from abuse and heinous crimes, and at the same time you will see others intent on imprisoning children's minds, exploiting their bodies sexually and engineering the destruction of the family which – under ideal conditions – is the ultimate "safe place" for a child. You will see great acts of kindness and gross acts of violence. You will see mindless and passive "sheep", and you will also see people driven into action with a passion never before experienced.

How would you assess all this, citizens of earth?

Do you simply sit back and say "There are two sides to every coin" or "It's always been like this" or "All this has nothing to do with me"? Are such observances a minor irritation to your otherwise smoothly running day, or are you continuously on edge as you discover more and more such examples, bringing you to an awareness that you are teetering on the edge of a precipice?

Do you look around you at all, Beloveds? Do you look at what is happening in other countries, looking beyond that which your media would have you believe? Do you look downwards, aware of new growth in the vegetation, and do you look upwards to see the increase in noctilucent clouds, or to gain a bigger picture? Do you have a "bird's eye view" of what is really going on?

To recognize the increasing DIVISION
in all aspects of life is to be increasingly aware of the
GREAT FALL, OF WHICH DIVISION IS A PREREQUISITE

It is as if two halves are irreconcilable, or permanently broken. And the initial reaction may be one of complete dismay, wondering whether the pieces can be glued back together.

Yet this is impossible because the "division" has occurred in so many different areas. This is not a clean break which can be easily healed: it is the complete shattering of all material into thousands of smithereens.

The only thing you can do is sweep them all up
and throw them away.

Following that, you can contemplate how to construct something new, providing that you can put emotions on hold, and providing you can get over the loss of something so familiar, however dreadful it may have been.

We warn you of the severity of the situation, and we urge you to continuously exercise your powers of critical awareness. That is to say: investigate the great good which humankind is capable of, as well as the great evil, for both exist, even if you have pushed the latter to the dark recesses of your mind. The "great evil" will inevitably resurface, and we do not want you to die as a result of this shock.

These are strong words, yet the situation is dire.
We observe you and only wish you the best.

Seraphin

Seraphin Message 483:
GUIDING LIGHTS AND CLEAN CORNERS

Through Rosie, 23rd February 2022

What does it mean to be a "guiding light", Beloveds?

If you are leading a party of like-minded individuals who are happy to follow in your footsteps and who are actually eager for guidance, being a guiding light is a very easy proposition. It will be fulfilling and even restful, because each person will automatically adjust to the pace of the other on your joint journey. Such followers will soak up wisdom and advice like a sponge, knowing that it will change their lives, knowing also that their failure to change themselves will mean a sudden "relapse" into unpleasant situations. They will know the importance of development, of pulling oneself out of the mud and of striving to reach new heights, and so anyone who provides valid instructions or who points the way will be openly and gratefully welcomed.

However, this is not the case on your world at the moment, except in select and mostly hidden groups – not hidden from themselves but from the public eye. The majority see no need for change; they are sinking slowly into a quagmire of their own making. They have an "I'll be damned if I am going to do anything about it" attitude. Many have turned to drink or substance abuse or continuous entertainment to stop the pain in its tracks. In fact, they do not even feel the pain any more in many cases, since they have shielded themselves so well against it.

Drugs, or films, or social media, or virtual realities have all played their own particular role in separating such persons from their ACTUAL REALITY, and their eyes are focused on these distractions only. If they work, they are actually always waiting for the moment when their "leisure time" starts, which they pack as full as possible with all sorts of self-deceiving activities, persuading themselves that everything is really alright.

Because of this intense focus on one direction, they never look into any "corners" to discover what is hidden there. These may hold old emotional wounds, old photographs, old memories, old habits, old convictions, and old broken relationships. All this is pushed aside into their subconscious, for they know that to clean out these corners would mean a lot of personal effort and a lot of personal pain. This they refuse to feel. The situation is coming when such hidden corners will be forcibly cleaned. This will arise due to an increase in "cosmic light" or cosmic energy.

But what is your position as a guiding light at this time? Guiding lights are generally uncomfortable for others. For those who hide from reality, you are a real threat. You uncover the lies which they have been consciously harbouring or which they have been hiding from themselves. You have been lighting up their "bad sides", their lack of virtue, their lack of dedication and their lack of morals. You make them feel as if they are on a "hot seat" plummeting down on a rollercoaster at great speed. This they want to avoid at all costs, so they avoid you. Thus, guiding lights are presently rejected, insulted, condemned as lunatics and isolated.

We would like to offer encouragement to you, the guiding lights. The cosmic energies will do their job, forcing more and more out into the open, and those who have refused to learn and who have refused to budge from their comfortable convictions and positions will soon appear en masse, feeling helpless, naked and often suicidal. This is where you come in; it will not be your role to reproach and laugh: it will be your role to be a guiding light, exactly as before, in order to help these traumatized people, helping them into the realization that not all is lost and that there is still (limited but enough) time to turn their behavior around and to dis-cover their own divinity and their own positive role in these dev-astating times.

You, as guiding lights, have an incredibly serious and important role to play. As the pressure of events increase exponentially, your area of expertise and the wisdom you have to offer will also be REQUIRED EXPONENTIALLY.

We encourage you to think about the enormity of your global predicament, and of the "weight" on your shoulders. And we would also remind you that YOU CAN DO IT.

YOU HAVE CHOSEN THIS ROLE LONG AGO,
AND CUMULATING PRESENT EVENTS ARE CONVERGING
INTO AN UNPRECEDENTED ACUTE SITUATION
IN WHICH YOU WILL BE SORELY NEEDED.

We love you, Seraphin

Seraphin Message 484:
EVERY THOUGHT SOUNDS THE COSMIC BELL

Through Rosie, 2nd March 2022

Not only does every thought sound the cosmic bell, Beloveds, but every breath is part of cosmic breath. What do we mean by using the word "cosmic"? We are not talking about vague or im-aginary "dimensions" as propagated in some of your new age philosophies. We are talking about very real physical space. We are talking about the whole universe (or "multiverse", as it con-tains millions of "universes"), and we are saying that the thoughts you have REVERBERATE THROUGHOUT THIS REALM. Your thoughts (to say nothing of your words and actions, which are a huge "magnification" of your thoughts, and even more powerful) are never "lost". They cannot be "swept under the carpet". They never "disappear in a puff of smoke". They are never untraceable. They can never be erased from "history". They are permanently written into the cosmic tapestry, recorded for all time, and they are universally accessible to those of a certain spiritual level.

The whole cosmos could be considered a book of thought which you have collectively written, and when we say "you" we do not only mean you personally, or you as the population of earth, but you as a member of the cosmic family, and you as EVERYONE WHO BELONGS TO THAT FAMILY. This will be too much for you to grasp: that you have trillions of cosmic brethren of all different shapes, sizes and colours, yet all infused with the same life force of the holy CREATION. These your brethren also have thoughts which reverberate eternally and affect every corner of the cosmos.

If you think of a certain person, your thought will travel to that person - its "target" - and will affect them, causing a change, however subtle. If those thoughts are of high quality, if they are compassionate and understanding, they will uplift the recipient. Such is the power of LOVE. Such is the power of what you call "prayer". It reaches into every corner of the multiverse and it can accomplish WONDERFUL THINGS.

If, however, those thoughts are violent and intend harm, the subject will receive a blow, however slight.

Realising this, and taking control of one's thoughts, tracking their patterns, discerning their negative and positive spiralling, is an extremely empowering process. Many of the thoughts you have are about YOURSELVES, so the quality of the thoughts about YOURSELVES will affect the health and vitality of YOURSELVES IN A POSITIVE OR NEGATIVE WAY, in accordance with WHAT EVER YOU CHOOSE TO THINK.

To give a very basic example, you will recover much more quickly from an illness if you repeatedly think I AM ON THE ROAD TO RECOVERY AND COMPLETE HEALTH. If you repeatedly think I AM ILL, this will have a negative impact.

You may now feel horrified to know that your every thought is tracked and recorded in cosmic vaults (and yes, there is technology capable of this). This may seem like "big brother watching you". This may seem like extreme surveillance and data collection. This may make you fearful. Yet this is not conducted by those who would control, manipulate and enslave you, as on your sorry planet. The purpose is more to understand sequences and to understand cause and effect. From such records, it is obvious to the reader why some things go wrong, and why others progress, in microcosms as well as macrocosms (and the multiverse is the ultimate macrocosm). Everything is clear. There are no mysteries. It constitutes a huge cosmic document of "real history", sometimes referred to on earth as the "Akashic records", though your grasp of the concept is extremely limited.

Imagine that you will, in the future, have access to this library of knowledge as a result of increased technology and increased spirituality (the latter is the prerequisite for increasing technology). And while we are on the subject of accessing certain "libraries" of information, the library donated by the avatar called Jesus is already available, if you should acknowledge that such transmissions are possible, and if you would strive to download such information to your own minds. (At this point we would like to add that some of you are already doing this subconsciously, and you refer to this as "intuition").

We have only touched here on a huge area of knowledge and scope which is unfamiliar to you. As such, this message is purely a pointer and cannot hope to cover the vast areas which are as yet unknown to you.

But perhaps it has given you an idea about WHAT YOU DO NOT KNOW. Hopefully, it has also indicated to you YOUR IMMENSE POWER TO INFLUENCE, and so we hope that you will exercise this power FOR THE BENEFIT OF ALL. Seraphin

Seraphin Message 485:
TO PANIC OR NOT TO PANIC: THAT IS THE QUESTION

Through Rosie, 16th March 2022

Even if you think you have got your lives in order, Citizens of Earth, and even if you are satisfied with your present way of life, and even if you have provided for the "future", and even if you are confident that your loved ones and friends are alright, let us remind you that the severity of what is coming will shock all of you, for no one is fully privy to the plans, both nefarious and holy.

It depends on your viewpoint and level of spirituality as to which plan you are presently focussing on. If fear rules your thoughts, then you will be constantly seeing the "crash" of various scenarios in the financial and material world. Things which used to run smoothly are simply not working the way they used to. Various procedures are breaking down. This is – among other things – because you have such a complex world in which the parts of a car or machine, for example, are manufactured in different corners of the world. If transport is "interrupted", it prevents the completion of the whole product.

On a different level, fear is gripping the minds of many, causing "irrational behaviours" which in turn affect all cycles, situations and relationships. Otherwise harmonious relationships – whether at home or at work – will come under immense pressure, and many will just crack under that same pressure due to a feeling of utter hopelessness and utter "doom". This means that they have seemingly come up against a DEAD END. They are not capable of looking sideways, or of stepping back and taking a new direction. They do not regard obstacles as deliberately placed circumstances which have the mission of propelling growth.

The potential learning curve is extremely steep at the moment. To step back from the wall requires immense courage, yet courage is what you will need if you intend to carry on here on earth.

Know that we are always watching you (we being your unseen guides) and we are already ready to catch you in our waiting arms IF YOU RECOGNISE OUR PRESENCE AND ASK.

For us, there is no such thing as a DEAD END.
There are only LIVING BEGINNINGS.

We never panic because we know that there is always a guiding hand available, and always a new perspective to gain. The learning journey is one of exhilaration, not of continual drudgery. Drudgery is experienced by those in a deep state of resignation.

Indeed, there is a lot which is occupying your minds, and which could contribute to this "spiralling down" of hope: there is war, and you fear it will spread to your own countries; there are riots, and you fear they will spread also. There are food shortages, there are serious environmental concerns, there are "mad politicians", and you might actually be quite convinced that the whole world is going mad and that everyone who does not panic and recognise this is some sort of "uncompassionate borg". In fact, it is the other way around. The "uncompassionate borgs" are those who have no inner divine connection, the ones who cannot step out of present negative mind-sets and who do not strive to learn, let alone to perfect themselves.

Can you remember a time when you fell into panic? Can you remember the overwhelming feeling of hopelessness and fear? Can you remember not being able to sleep at night? Can you remember certain thoughts constantly dominating your day? Compassion for anyone in this state is to be brought to the table, however it should be combined with taking the affected person by the hand and showing them that there is another perspective. What is most missing is the DIVINE PERSPECTIVE – that we are never abandoned, even in our darkest moments, even when everything is about to collapse, even when we cower in the last hole. We reiterate very strongly here that you are in DIVINE HANDS.

Cumulating events are putting you to the test, and this will get much stronger. We would like to remind you that you have a CHOICE whether to panic or not. To panic or not to panic is related to Shakespeare's speech TO BE OR NOT TO BE, which might be interpreted as TO BE OR NOT TO BE SOVEREIGN. Hamlet is pondering the ills of life, and wondering whether it is not better to die. Your choices today are the same: TO LIVE OR NOT TO LIVE, and this does not depend on outward circumstances but on spiritual maturity.

To panic is to FORGET WHO YOU REALLY ARE,
which is an AGENT OF THE DIVINE.

Remember this in the dark period which is to come. You will be presented with myriad opportunities to help others, and you cannot do this if you are in a paralysed and panicky state. It is with great sadness that we gaze upon the struggles which will inevitably ensue, but we also rejoice that great leaps of learning will be taken which will ultimately benefit you.

Seraphin

PART 2

THE PIONEER EXERCISE MANUAL

What is a pioneer? Pioneers relish problems and possess the ability to thrive in difficult circumstances. They forge ahead regardless of all barriers, fuelled sometimes by idealism and always by a sense of adventure. Stranded in the middle of a desert, they will find some way to build a shelter. Placed on another planet, they will build a new community. Caught in the middle of a disaster, wherever it is, they will pick up the pieces. Pioneers have many positive qualities – determination, optimism, strength of character and focus. However, if they give reign to ego or self-interest, pioneers can also turn into insensitive and exploitative slave drivers.

There is no doubt that there is a great need for pioneers on this planet. In the coming scenarios which will involve great loss of life, widespread physical damage, the crumbling of society and the invalidation of many "world views", pioneers will be required for immediate action, whether this means rebuilding and reorganizing, or helping to deal with trauma. And they themselves will not be excluded from this trauma. They will be impelled to **strive for unity**, as described in Seraphin Message 406 below.

The following exercises have been inspired by Seraphin to help pioneers of the new earth, to support their much-needed pioneer passion, to warn of the pitfalls, and to assist a smooth transition to the state of "light and life" which is our planet's destiny. Pioneers are presented with many questions so that they can better understand themselves and others, so that their contribution is more effective. The real work, then, is carried out in the minds of you, the pioneers who are reading this. The questions are merely a catalyst for self-development and can be applied to any project, past, present or future.

It is ultimately this - self-development and the recognition that we are all divine co-creators - which will put the planet back on track. It is the sad lack of such self-awareness, in combination with a cultivated lack of compassion and lack of critical thinking, which have necessitated this winding down of our violent and decadent "civilisation". For millennia, this burden of negativity has been weighing down on earth, with the result that she cannot deal with it any more. Thus, she has decided – as a sentient being on her own spiritual path - to initiate a new beginning.

Seraphin Message 406: STRIVING FOR UNITY

Through Rosie. 1st April 2020

Dear inhabitants of earth who are presently going through a period of intense suffering. This is how you perceive it – a period of quarantine during which you are not allowed to continue with your day-to-day living and familiar faces.

But unbeknown to you, Beloveds of the ONE CREATION, you have been in a period of quarantine for thousands of years as a planet, separated from your galactic neighbours and the harmonious circuit of universe administration which could have provided so much assistance and solace during your tribulations.

This "cutting of" was initiated by YOURSELVES (or we can say EARLIER INCARNATIONS OF YOURSELVES). It was a deliberate attempt on your part to escape universal law, to set yourselves above it, to abdicate responsibility, to "go it alone", to forge ahead without considering your effect or response, to detach yourselves as your own gods, and to see others as "less".

Over millennia, these criminals have dominated your society, holding the rest of you – weakened and manipulated – in their sway, using all thinkable, unthinkable and devious methods to keep you IN THE DARK.

Yet the laws of balance are always in play, and if the pendulum has swung for millennia towards the dark – involving some of the most heinous and horrible crimes against humanity – then it must necessarily redress that movement and SWING TOWARDS THE LIGHT.

You see, the cosmic laws are simple, effective and ALWAYS KICK IN WHEN THE LIMIT HAS BEEN REACHED, just as you yourselves will explode in anger if you have been struggling to be patient for a long time. When you reach "boiling point", there is no retreating. When the scales are tipped, there is no "going back".

Some of you naively think that – following this period of hiatus – you will return to life as it was – that you will return to "normal", but this would defy cosmic law. Cycles must be completed. Closure and DEATH of degenerate behaviour is a requisite for new growth. Fear must be felt, in order to return to LOVE. Separation must be experienced in full, in order to RETURN TO COMPLETE UNITY.

Your overlords have – over the ages – designed so many constructs to keep you separate – nation against nation, man against woman, political party against political party, caste against caste, human against animals (yes, you mistreat, kill and eat them), and individual against individual, striving for power.

WHEN ALL THIS IS OVER (and we can assure you that all this depravity and misuse of your "independence" will soon be over, including the removal of your dark overlords who furthered it) WHAT WILL YOU STRIVE FOR NEXT?

The trauma of ultimately discovering the true, sordid nature of your SEPARATION, and of discovering the inhuman torturing and cannibalistic nature of those who have led you by the nose, will be very difficult to bear.

Many will not be able to bear it – not being of courageous, pioneer material - and will depart for other realms (the process you erroneously call "death", for it simply means "life elsewhere", a new task to fulfil and a new role to play).

Those who remain will STRIVE FOR THE OPPOSITE. All fences of separation, which have been supported with immense clout and financial power over the ages, WILL FALL, leaving you with an intense, continually burning DESIRE TO UNIFY.

It is this monumental force which will reshape your personal lives, your communities, your nations and your world. It will permeate all thinking, all discussions and all proceedings.

Do you see now, citizens of earth, why this present PERIOD OF SEPARATION IS CRITICAL? It may seem to be connected to a completely different scenario – that of spreading disease – but it is actually specifically designed to make you come to your senses and to experience – with your own bodies and minds – the PAIN OF SEPARATION.

"How is this possible?" you may ask. You are caught up in the web of propaganda which has fuelled this deplorable condition on earth for an immensely long period of time. The perfidy and attention to detail which your controllers employ, has schooled you well. To inform you of the existence of benevolent galactic forces, with all the details, would just be brushed off by you with a smile and a dismissive wave of the hand – so completely have you been brainwashed, so completely have you been duped.

This carpet of lies is about to be pulled out from under your feet. REJOICE, for this cycle is necessarily coming to an end, and your role in the new "landscape", cleansed of filth and corruption, will be a sometimes painful but ultimately glorious passage.

We will stop here with this message – this scribe is running out of paper – and you are running out of time. AWAKE, ASSESS YOUR QUALITIES, RECOGNISE YOUR MISTAKES AND STEP OUT BOLDLY INTO A GLORIOUS FUTURE. Seraphin.

COPING WITH CRISES

Earth is entering a very intense stage of her history, and her citizens are faced with unprecedented crisis as well as an unprecedented chance to rectify and redirect the "impasse" or dead end to which all human activities have so far led. This means acquiring deep insights leading to beneficial changes in behaviour, as well as physical actions based on newly acquired principles.

These necessary rectifications may, at the beginning, completely overwhelm you, despite your intrinsic pioneer spirit. It may seem almost impossible at first to bear this burden, because there is so much to do. Yet each individual has unique qualities and skills. These must be encouraged and implemented, step by step, minute by minute, everyone concentrating on their own field of expertise, and resting in between.

Exercise

Please close your eyes and ask a friend to read this to you very slowly, leaving very long pauses between every sentence so that the listener has a chance to visualise all the details.

Imagine you going on a very long journey by car to a very nice destination. Choose some people to go with you. You are full of excitement, though some of the journey might be difficult. Plan the journey and the nice breaks carefully in your mind, according to your great expectations. Imagine yourself setting off and talking to your fellow companions in the car. Everything is going well. Now you get caught in a traffic jam and there is a danger of being stuck in one place for hours if you don't make a decision. You disagree. A severe storm with massive hailstones ensues. Then you encounter a pleasant surprise. Then you encounter another setback. Then you help someone. Fog descends and you can't see anything. Then someone helps you. Then you arrive at your destination. You recover and celebrate. The next day you wake up and reflect on the whole experience, reliving all details of it in your mind. You watch how the influence of this experience affects your behaviour during the next week.

Then open your eyes and answer the following questions:

QUESTIONS

Did you feel like a pioneer, some of the time, or all of the time?

How did your fixed expectations differ from reality?

Did your expectations about what would be difficult turn out to be easy?

Did your expectations about what would be easy turn out to be difficult?

Would it have been easier to deal with if you had travelled with an open mind?

Did you take enough breaks to reflect upon any difficult situations?

Did you choose a course of action and discover it was a mistake?

Did you try to relieve the stress of your fellow travellers?

Did you lose your nerve at any stage?

If you ever felt desperate, did you communicate that?

Was there ever a stage when you just wanted to give it all up and turn back home?

Did you take any risks?

How did you relieve tension on arrival?

Did you cause any risk to yourself on arrival through compensating for the unpleasant experiences of your journey?

Did you praise and encourage your companions for "holding out"?

Did you take the opinions of your fellow travellers seriously?

How long did the after-effects of stress last?

Did you take time to rest, or did you rush into the next "tension-filled" activity?

Did you enjoy any of your journey?

Did your journey involve any pleasant moments, or is your memory of the journey dominated by long stretches of uncertainty?

Did you ever think you were on the wrong road, but later discovered that it was the right route after all?

Were you ever convinced that you were on the right road, when actually it was the wrong one?

CLEARING A BLOCKED PATH

Pioneers will be called upon in all sorts of emergencies. Clearing "paths" of all sorts must be undertaken on a massive scale. How will this be done?

Exercise

Please close your eyes and ask a friend to read this to you very slowly, leaving very long pauses between every sentence so that the listener has a chance to visualise all the details.

Imagine that you are standing in front of a very long, thorny jungle path, which has not been used for many years. It leads to a wonderful, life-giving river where you would like to swim. How are you going to set about the task of clearing the path? It will take many days. It will involve a lot of surprises both pleasant and unpleasant. While working, you discover something beautiful. What do you do about it? While working, you discover objects which suggest that you are not the first to walk this path. What do you do with them? While working, you find something dangerous. How do you react? You run into problems. Take enough time to visualise all stages of the whole path-clearing process from beginning to end. How do you feel, now that the work is completed? What do you do next?

Then open your eyes and answer the following questions:

QUESTIONS

Did you set out on your task immediately, or did sit down and reflect upon how you were going to approach this?

Did you contemplate involving other people in your plan?

Did the plan involve any co-creation or co-operation?

Did you put on special gloves or clothing in order to protect yourself against thorns?

Did you take the right tools with you, or were they too small, too powerful, too destructive, or not effective enough?

Did you carry out "tabula rasa", or did you leave foliage or stones or interesting features still standing to serve as reminders, or to arouse interest, or to preserve beauty?

Did you, in your great desire to reform and clear the path, destroy something valuable or beautiful?

Did you, in your desire to make quick progress, stumble over something unseen and hurt yourself?

Did you cut the branches so that the path could only accommodate one person going forward,
or was it for two people, or was it for a car or other vehicle?

Did you consider future generations as you forged your way ahead, or did you do this purely for your own satisfaction,
or in order to fulfil a given task?

What did you do with the thorny branches?

Did you throw them to the side, or well out of the way,
or did you remove them to another place to be burnt?

Is there any possibility that the thorns left near the path will fall back onto it in the next storm?

Did you discover traces of those who had been there before you, and who have tried to do the same work, but who failed to do so, or who committed some mistake, or did not complete the course, or took "short cuts" which left problems in their wake?

Did you have to clear up these problems which others left behind?

Do you recognize where they went wrong?

Will this help you to avoid making similar mistakes in the future?

Have you left any problems behind you for the next pioneers to solve?

What is the benefit of leaving a non-perfect path behind you?

Does it open up opportunities for others to become creative?

Did you eliminate the roots of the thorny plants, or did you just cut them off?

Did you stop in awe when you saw something beautiful?

Did you recognize when to stop cutting away at stubborn roots, realising that roots on slopes are necessary to hold the ground together and to stop stones from falling?

Did you remove structures which caused immediate damage?

Did you find any rubbish on the way?

Did you take it away with you?

Did you sometimes look behind you to see if there was anything you have missed?

Did you take a rest in between?

Did you celebrate at the end?

Was the destination what you expected?

Were you happy with the way things went?

What could have been done better?

DEALING WITH DAMAGE

As a pioneer, you will be called upon to deal with all sorts of physical damage in areas of expertise where you may have little experience. You may be put in situations you have never encountered before.

Exercise

Please close your eyes and ask a friend to read this to you very slowly, leaving very long pauses between every sentence so that the listener has a chance to visualise all the details.

Imagine that you live in a rural area which has been hit very hard by violent weather conditions. It leaves a hundred houses in your village with extreme damage and no electricity. Emergency services are strained to the limit. You decide to gather group of volunteers, but many are too scared to go into action. How do you start to deal with this situation? How will you cook? How will you keep warm? Take time to visualize a storm, all the effects it has and the measures you decide to initiate to counteract all the damage done. You encounter set-backs. You encounter successes. Decide on your short-term and long-term actions and carry them out until life has returned to some "normality".

Then open your eyes and answer the following questions:

QUESTIONS

Did you manage to gather enough support?

Did you try and include all villagers in the process?

Did you encourage everyone to share resources?

Did you find the right words to encourage others to volunteer?

Did you implement permanent or temporary solutions?

Did you sometimes resort to quick solutions?

Did you cover up damage rather than treating it immediately?

Did you deal with symptoms or eliminate causes?

Did you protect sensitive areas against future storms?

Did you contemplate the recovery capabilities of nature, or did you immediately discard plants or "growing things" which were destroyed or broken?

Did you celebrate your co-creative efforts?

OVERCOMING TRAUMA

As a pioneer, you will be dealing with people who have lost very important aspects of their lives, as well as loved ones.

Exercise

Please close your eyes and ask a friend to read this to you very slowly, leaving very long pauses between every sentence so that the listener has a chance to visualise all the details.

Imagine that everyone is suffering trauma. You can include yourself in this. Due to the release of important, radical and undeniable information, your whole view of the world, as well as of your own particular role in it, has changed. All this has resulted in mental and physical paralysis. How do you deal with this? As a pioneer, visualize what strategies you will develop to help the following people in need:

People who have lost their loved ones
People who have lost their jobs
People who have lost their dreams
People who have lost their egos
People who have lost their self-respect
People who have lost their convictions
People who have lost their life's purpose
People who have lost their saviours and religions
People who have lost their trust
People who have lost their scapegoats
People who have lost their habits of convenience
People who have lost their and methods of self-comfort.

Take enough time to visualize your counteractions
and their results.

Then open your eyes and answer the following questions:

QUESTIONS

As a pioneer, do you sometimes lose sympathy with those who seem paralysed?

Can you remember a time when you felt absolutely paralysed?

What was the cause?

When did you last lose a loved one and what effect did it have on you?

How long did it take before you managed to go into action?

Even if you are presently unaffected, can you sympathise with those who are in a state of despair?

Can you recognize the fine line where you may start to "over-sympathise?"

Are you able to pick the right moment to stop sympathizing?

Can you assess when someone is ready to take on a small task?

Can you assess when someone is ready to take on a large task?

Is it clear to you that all feelings must be processed?

Is it clear that failure to process all feelings will, in the long run, restrict progress on the new earth?

FLEXIBILITY AND ROLE CHANGE

In a world full of broken structures where life cannot continue "as usual", pioneers may suddenly find themselves in violently fluctuating circumstances which they do not have completely under control. In such situations, the ability to ask for help or adopt a different role may be paramount, and while you may try to make plans, you can never be certain that this will come to fruition in the way you have imagined. Thus, flexibility is required.

Exercise

Please close your eyes and ask a friend to read this to you very slowly, leaving very long pauses between every sentence so that the listener has a chance to visualise all the details.

Imagine that you are expecting a lot of visitors to stay overnight. You spend a long time preparing everything for them. You encounter some problems. You manage to solve them. At the last minute, without any notice, you discover that they are all going to stay somewhere else instead. Take time to visualize this situation and your reaction.

Then open your eyes and answer the following questions:

QUESTIONS

Do you "let go" easily?

If not, what is stopping you?

Is being a host associated with your ego?

How quickly can you readjust to a different pace or place or experience?

Can you deal easily with being a leader or pioneer one moment, and a "follower" the next?

Do you feel "demoted" by this?

Can you rise easily from follower to leader?

Does this inflate your ego?

Do you play many roles, moving easily and fluidly between them, or are you fixed in one particular role?

PIONEER INTERACTIONS

Creating the "new world" will not be the result of leaders directing everyone else. Its ultimate success will rest on co-creative efforts, and thus you are asked to reflect on how well you relate to others, and how well you can work together towards a common goal.

Exercise

Please close your eyes and ask a friend to read this to you very slowly, leaving very long pauses between every sentence so that the listener has a chance to visualise all the details.

Imagine that you are suddenly designated manager of a very worthwhile project which is dear to your heart. It is such a big project that you have to invite others to become involved. These are your first impressions: some are very enthusiastic non-professionals who want to storm ahead without much planning.

Some are idealists and refuse to compromise. Some seem to be in it for the money. Some tend to "tell tales" about each other. Some use charm and seduction for their own advantage. Others appear to have considerable expertise but are not keen on sharing. All this results in conflicts which require solutions. Take enough time to imagine in detail your interactions and meetings with these different groups of people who are all necessary for the project. At last, after a much dedication, the project is successfully completed.

Then open your eyes and answer the following questions:

QUESTIONS

Did you rely on first impressions alone?

Did you allow for the fact that others are developing, just as you are developing?

Were your first impressions coloured by your own likes and dislikes?

If someone gossiped about a colleague, were you automatically on your guard, or did you come to your own conclusions?

Were you easily swayed by a smile or a pretty face or a compliment?

How authentic was your own behaviour?

Did you act like the person "in command"?

Did you make apologies or reject compliments to make others feel better?

Did you have the patience to let others tell their story?

Did you have the presence to interrupt a narrative which was irrelevant, repetitive or demotivating?

Did you strive to include all participants in conversation?

Did you allow someone to dominate, while others remain silent?

Were you good at being the co-ordinator?

Did you notice when others were burning to say something which is relevant?

Did you allow ego games to continue?

Did you see colleagues as sheep temporarily in your fold?

Did you forget your needs, or those of your colleagues?

Did you give them a break?

Did you retire before you were at the end of your strength?

Were you able to put yourself in their shoes?

Did you introduce humour to make people feel at ease?

Did you gravitate towards those who agreed with you?

Did you accept help from others?

Did you lay out any structure for discussion?

When the project was finished, how did you feel?

Did you feel proud of yourself?

Did you express pride in your team of co-creators?

Did the process expand your horizons?

WORKING IN TEAMS

It must be clear that students and teachers are essential to each other. Neither can function without the other. The next very important realization is that teachers are SIMULTANEOUSLY students, and students are SIMULTANEOUSLY teachers. Teachers learn to teach with each new student.

Exercise

Please close your eyes and ask a friend to read this to you very slowly, allowing for a fair amount of time between every sentence so that the person conducting the exercise is able to build up this picture in their mind.

Imagine that you are member of a large team which is rebuilding a section of society which has been completely decimated. Decide what that section is and develop detailed plans for it. You will have a team of ten people, all with a different area of expertise, and with different ranges of skill. Select your candidates for your team. Together, you will mutually assist each other and put completely new structures in place. Interaction is required on all levels for many months. There are daily sessions in which everyone shares their feelings and experiences. You monitor and contribute to such sessions. Problems arise. Some team members do not get along. After many discussions, plans and setbacks, your original goal is achieved and celebrated.

Open your eyes and answer the following questions:

QUESTIONS

What stance did you maintain in your interactions?

Did you recognize the fine line between helping someone and discouraging their independence?

Did you take setbacks personally?

Did you listen well?

If someone was relating their experience, did you immediately interrupt after one sentence to present them with your own story, relating a similar or a different experience?

Did your eagerness to communicate your side of the story obliterate your compassion?

Did you take a break when it was all too much for you?

Did you take a break without informing others, leaving others in the lurch?

Were you easily depressed by lack of instant success?

Were you continually on the lookout for others?

Were you worried that others may not be getting along with each other?

Did you expend energy worrying?

Did you feel responsible for everyone, always building diplomatic bridges between them?

Did you see everything as a stage leading towards another stage?

Did you insist on perfection?

Were you aware of the fact that sub-optimal solutions allow others to make suggestions and grow?

How would you have reacted if a member of your team fell ill?

Would you have resented the fact that they can now "opt out" of work?

Is your attention towards weaker members of your team constant or sporadic?

Would you have felt guilty if you fell ill?

Did you at any point recognize that you were being manipulated by others?

Did you truly share your own emotional experiences at the end of each day?

BUILDING COMMUNITY CENTRES

Isolation and loneliness has been a major problem so for many members of society. There is also an urgent need for places where ideas can be exchanged. How will pioneers rectify this?

Exercise

Please close your eyes and ask a friend to read this to you very slowly, leaving very long pauses between every sentence so that the listener has a chance to visualise all the details.

Imagine that you are encouraged to follow your passions. Your passion and your skills result in designing a large centre (whether social, medical, commercial, agricultural, environmental, cultural etc.) which will benefit many, and which also requires the co-operation of a lot of people. It is the very best project you can imagine. Where will this be built? What do you need for it to be successful? You have all available resources. You are in charge and you get up every morning to work on this project. Your colleagues have vastly different skills, motivations and backgrounds. You hold meetings attended by them all. You begin the project in the spring, and you end it in the autumn. In winter, you present it to the public. You encounter difficulties along the way due to incompatible visions and practicalities. You experience mutiny. You experience a necessary change in plan. Unexpected twists and turns result in some people leaving. Other aspects are successful. Take time to trace this project from the "drawing board" to the very end.

Then open your eyes and answer the following questions:

QUESTIONS

Did you select the ideal location?

If not, what were the advantages and disadvantages of the place you selected?

Was there any conflict between organisers, builders and employees?

Was the complete plan clear to everyone working on it?

Were "experts" or specialists in their field able to communicate their expertise in a way in which others could understand?

Was there any use of "jargon" which prevented clarity?

Did you, as the project's designer, manage to retain an overview of developments?

Did the project turn out as originally planned?

Was that a good or a bad thing?

Were there any hiccups in the proceedings?

Were there any unexpected challenges?

Did the workers, or you, suddenly refuse to continue?

If so, what was the reason?

If you made a mistake, could you admit it to your colleagues?

Were you quick to make someone or something else responsible?

How happy were you to take over responsibility, even when something failed?

Could you apologise?

If you were overworked, did you make this known?

If there were problems, did unconditional love come into the equation?

Were you true to your word?

Did you twist the trust so that it fitted in with your narrative?

Were you reliable and punctual?

How did any supposed "negative" traits slow the project down?

What did you do if social activities like "talking on the job" slowed down the whole process for others?

If your colleague had a fascinating personality and many skills, did this persuade you to overlook their negligence?

If a co-creator was older and physically compromised, did you expect the same effort?

Did you emphasise that each individual should contribute in their unique way?

How did you feel on completion of the project?

What did you learn during the project?

What would you change in view of your experience if you were ask to lead another project of this kind?

PART 3

THE WORLD WILL BECOME PEACEFUL, BEAUTIFUL AND ABUNDANT

This is the name of a book already published in 2020 (Book 4 in the Seraphin Series), yet over the last couple of years I have continued to telepathically receive similar brief "pearls of wisdom" inspired by Seraphin. These "continuations" are printed here.

As before, they focus on our personal, social, cultural, global, environmental and DIVINE RESPONSIBILITIES. As before, they are extremely confident in tone and assure us that IF we adopt these new forms of behaviour, there is no doubt that we will co-create a peaceful, beautiful and abundant world.

The world will become peaceful, beautiful and abundant
IF WE REMEMBER THAT THERE IS
ALWAYS A DIVINE PLAN

Here is some advice for you: by all means, take precautions to protect yourself, and always remain aware, knowing that what is actually put out in the media may be the exact opposite of what is really going on. This is a great testing time, during which it is clear that those who fall into despair have no real idea about THE DIVINE PLAN. You may rest assured that there is a DIVINE PLAN, and that galactic observers are watching the situation closely, and are intervening where necessary. If there is standstill in your thinking, and especially if there is standstill in your hearts, you will not be able to perceive the "chinks" in the wall – a wall with which the majority are confronted at the moment. The clouds will recede, and then you will see the purpose of all this, and why the situation was allowed to develop in this way. It has a higher purpose. This will be clear at the END of the story.

The world will become peaceful, beautiful and abundant
IF PEACE IS LIVED RATHER THAN RESURRECTION
BEING REPEATEDLY CELEBRATED

Why is good Friday called GOOD?

It is celebrating the DELIBERATE MURDER of an enlightened master whose aim it was to awaken people to the INNER GOD INSIDE YOU. And it is this "lack of awakening" which is continu-ing to allow wars and violence to continue. Celebrating Easter with eggs and rabbits refers back to spring rituals of fertility. The supposed "resurrection" of Jesus has been rolled into it.

The question is: why celebrate death and new life once a year in this way? What about every day? What about continuous respect for all life? What about continuous awareness of PROGRESS (and death is only another form of progress) in every second? Is this what Jesus or any messenger of his calibre would have wanted? Would he recommend yearly enactments of his crucifixion, or daily dedication to acting in a way which promotes peace and embodies compassion?

**The world will become peaceful, beautiful and abundant
IF WE CLEARLY RECOGNISE WHEN OUR HUMANITY
IS BEING DELIBERATELY CURTAILED**

When, in the history of our countries, has it been explicitly forbidden that children visit their parents, and that families come together? When have hugs been outlawed? When have relatives been prevented from visiting dying family in hospitals? Are you aware of the experiments conducted on children to see whether they survive without human touch? They do not survive. Is it not time to rise up and expose this attempt to crush you? It is not time to visit those who need it? Is it not time to show those who organized this that their "experiment" to see how docile you are, has not actually worked? Will fear prevent you from loving? Are you content to remain isolated, so that you cannot receive - or more importantly - cannot give love?

**The world will become peaceful, beautiful and abundant
IF WE ARE PREPARED TO REVISE OUR CONVICTIONS**

Those who will fare best through this very intense period of confusion and chaos, followed by astounding and also disturbing revelations, will be people who can say OH; IT SEEMS THAT I WAS WRONG. SO WHERE DO WE GO FROM HERE? Those who are not able to "release" their convictions, their fondest hopes, their life-long "mental companions", their firmly founded structures or organizations, will suddenly stagnate, or even die, because their version of life, or their worldview, is crumbling around their ears, and they will not be able to bear it. What is the degree of suffering you can take?

Is it clear that this is just holding on to that which is obsolete, corrupt and desecrating?

Is it not a huge relief to know that - however dreadful the past may have been - you are moving forward to a new era?

This is simply a warning that everyone on earth will be faced with these challenges, and that you all have a choice whether to move on, or to remain stuck.

The world will become peaceful, beautiful and abundant
IF WE DO NOT LOSE HOPE

This is a time of great "rethinking" due to chaotic situations and due to being deprived of familiar circumstances, contacts and friends. Do not give in to negative thoughts that this will last a long time. It is temporary. It is a chance to discover without a doubt what we hold dear in our lives and what has genuine worth. It is also a time to recuperate and gather strength, because we are going to need it in the future in order to rebuild our world with the visions we develop now.

May we use this disturbing and deliberately exacerbated "hiatus" to gain more awareness of what has been going "wrong" for thousands of years, and - with this new knowledge - create a society where everyone's behaviour is compassed by love for their neighbour.

The world will become peaceful, beautiful and abundant
IF WE DO NOT FALL INTO HELPLESSNESS
AT THE SIGHT OF VIOLENCE

At the present time, there is much unprecedented violence flaring up around the world. Some will react by throwing their hands into the air and will be saturated with a feeling of helplessness. They will be in shock that something so terrible could happen "out of the blue". They may feel paralyzed and unable to do anything.

Everything is governed by the cosmic law of cause and effect, from the smallest surprise to the largest incident. To react with helplessness is to have forgotten that there is an original cause for this violence. If this fact is recognized, it may spur people on to investigate into the very roots of human behaviour, into the untrodden corners of human history, into the world of propaganda and manipulation which has been governing our planet for millennia. This is our chance; to dig out the cause. If we cannot do this, then we cannot reverse it. If we only recognize superficial causes, then we can only carry out superficial changes. It is our task to take on this responsibility.

The world will become peaceful, beautiful and abundant
IF WE REALISE THAT OUR HAPPINESS
IS NOT DEPENDENT ON OTHERS

So many people look outside of themselves for their pleasures, content, inspiration and comfort. This leads to a state of dependency, to whatever small or large degree. This means that you have not recognized yourself as an intricately functioning and amazing human being full of limitless potential, and if you have not recognized this YOURSELF, no recognition or force from outside will be able to make you realize the truth of this. So, you find yourselves in a vicious circle, requiring outward impetus to secure inward content.

Are outside forces so strong that you would forget your inner worth? Do you want to feel like froth being tossed on the top of the waves of a raging ocean, never finding peace until you die (rest in peace!). Even if this is your perspective, know that it does not end there - life continues in another form - and there the same challenge awaits you - the recognition of yourselves as divine beings.

The world will become peaceful, beautiful and abundant
IF WE KNOW THAT WE CAN NEVER
KNOW ANOTHER PERSON

If we find ourselves saying "Oh, I never thought you would ever say that!" or "I've never seen you like this before" or indeed "I cannot believe this is happening" or "Never in my life would I have imagined that this is now going on", then this is a major invitation to look at these sentences and discover that they are actually the expression of someone who has ALREADY ASSUMED THAT THEY KNOW PRECISELY HOW SOMEONE THINKS, OR WHY SOMETHING HAPPENS.

If we have a fixed, preconceived idea about how someone is, then we are completely disregarding the fact that we only have access to a certain part of their existence, and only part access to their thoughts or their past. We are also ignoring that we only see what we recognize, or what hits us, or what triggers us. To have a fixed idea of someone is also rejecting the idea that they might be on a their own very personal learning journey, changing from moment to moment.

Regarding our ideas about certain situations; here also, we cannot KNOW FOR SURE. We can assess certain incidents, and we can choose to research them or not. We can choose to accept without question what other people say about them. We can, if we are willing, add up small pieces of information or experience which might make a "mosaic" of our own version of the "TRUTH". THOSE PEOPLE WHO BEST SURVIVE THIS VERY DIFFI-CULT PERIOD WILL BE THE FLEXIBLE THINKERS. THEY WILL BE ABLE TO SAY "OH, IT SEEMS THAT I WAS WRONG ABOUT THIS. NEVER MIND. LET'S HAVE ANOTHER LOOK". Those that cannot revise their versions of events, or their view of others, will fare badly. If everyone worldwide adopts this learning stance, progress in all areas will be rapid.

The world will become peaceful, beautiful and abundant
IF WE ARE PREPARED TO STARE EVIL IN THE FACE

This is something that we will all have to do at some stage, if we want to rid this planet of the evil which has beset her for millennia. This is no easy journey. For those people who are led mainly by compassion, their first instinct when hearing about or seeing hei-nous crimes of the very worst sort imaginable, will be to turn away screaming, or to fall to the ground and faint. This is understand-able. This does not fit into the world they want to see.

However, we are not presently concerned with the world we want to see, although it is extremely important to uphold ideals for the future. What we are dealing with at the moment, is the reality in front of us - a world saturated by Satanism, destructive agendas and corrupted politics, with a purpose to do us harm. This must be stopped. And it cannot be stopped if we cannot deal with look-ing at it full on.

This may involve seeing something which cannot be "unseen". This may be realizing that the unthinkable has happened "on our watch". This is extremely painful. Some will survive it, and some will not, yet LOOKING AT IT ALL is essential to our collective forward progress. When we have a complete grasp of the depth of the depravity, we then have sufficient insight to develop the tools to create the opposite.

The world will become peaceful, beautiful and abundant IF WE WATCH OURSELVES WHILE WATCHING OUTWARD CIRCUMSTANCES

There are those who would have us believe that it is our job just to forge ahead, from one pay check to the next, from one "success" to the next, in a world where material possessions and outward appearance (eternally youthful) counts for more than anything else. But we are actually born naked, and will leave this world naked. The inner experience, and the wisdom attained through initiating, is what we actually TAKE WITH US. All other "baggage" falls away.

In these difficult times, what we see outside of ourselves is a macrocosm of what is happening inside of ourselves. It will serve us well to discover where these parallels exist. If we see dishonesty on the political scene, we are invited to search out the dishonesty in the little ways we avoid telling the truth in our relationships with others. If we see large-scale waste of resources, we are invited to acknowledge our own (however minuscule) failings to reuse or recycle. And if we see the world stagnating, for whatever reason, we are invited to ask ourselves how our views, our beliefs, our convictions, our relationships and our behaviours are in "stagnation" and "unchangeable". If everyone does this, positive change is inevitable.

**The world will become peaceful, beautiful and abundant
IF WE STOP USING FORCE**

Sometimes, when we are conversing with friends or acquaintances, we feel a great amount of tension arising within ourselves because we feel something very keenly, or because we have a wonderful suggestion to make, or because we have essential information to impart, and we feel like we may explode because we cannot find a "window" to express ourselves in a fast-moving conversation dominated by other individuals. We cannot find a gap to jump in. In the end, we may become so frustrated that we blurt out something which is not relevant to that being discussed, with a vehemence which surprises or shocks.

This is a situation involving violence on both sides. Those dominating are not aware of the needs / feelings / potential of those who wish to speak. They are not aware of the force they are exerting. Those who wish to speak but cannot, are not aware of the force they are imposing, once they do make use of a "window".

How can this use of violence be avoided? "Dominant" superiors may develop a greater sensitivity to those surrounding them, allowing them increased participation. Those who wish to participate more should learn to express themselves at earlier stages, before they feel impelled to burst in with their information. They are invited to become more confident, but also they are also invited to recognize whether their contribution is actually relevant to the discussion, rather than just a release of pent-up energies. They may need to become more serene and selfless, letting go of things which are not important to the whole. Thus can the use of force, which manifests at its extreme level in wars between nations, be avoided.

**The world will become peaceful, beautiful and abundant
IF WE LISTEN TO EACH OTHER FULLY INSTEAD OF
LAUNCHING INTO OUR OWN AGENDA**

Sometimes we may have a burning desire to pursue a goal, and if only ourselves are involved, we can rage ahead, feeling a great surge of satisfaction at our progress. However, most projects and goals involve the cooperation of other people, and they may be at various stages of development, or have varying degrees of enthusiasm, depending on their present circumstances.

It is these circumstances of which we must ideally be aware before we attempt to move ahead together in the direction of a common goal. Imagine that we meet as a group to achieve a common goal, such as organizing an event or simply meeting to sing or play. If one member of the group has just suffered a major setback, or has lost a relative, then how can we simply continue as if nothing has happened?

This would mean that the person concerned has to hold back their emotions, has to pretend that everything is alright. How many people in the world at this moment are holding back their emotions? What happens individually also happens globally.

The situation is dire: deep emotions remain unexpressed and the majority pretend that everything is alright. They simply continue with what is prescribed. Thus, mass awakening is so very necessary. In the end, "normal" agendas cannot continue due to this huge build-up of non-expression, self-deception, ignorance and compliance which has allowed evil to reign.

**The world will become peaceful, beautiful and abundant
IF WE PLAY CLOSE ATTENTION TO NATURE
AND FULFIL OUR OWN BLUEPRINT**

Without the human being, which has interrupted nature's DIVINE PLAN, many situations which are presently "out of hand" or diffi-cult to control would not have arisen. It is our mandate to live AS PART OF NATURE as opposed to taking on the position of some superior being who is directing the stage, killing animals as they see fit, exploiting natural resources at will, and rearranging the landscape to fit the human agenda.

The agenda is pivotal: nature has one (as do we all) and it is our task to fulfil it to the best of our ability. Then will true abundance be achieved.

Consider the plant Euphorbia lathyris which is most astonishing in its growth. It starts out as a completely straight stem, sprouting 4 leaves at regular intervals. It is completely in balance. It stretches towards the sky. It does not yet give any hint of the flower or seeds it may produce.

After growing upwards for a long time, there is a SUDDEN CHANGE TO MOVE IN THE DIRECTION OF ABUNDANCE, AND INSTEAD OF STRIVING IN ONE DIRECTION ONLY, THE STEM DIVIDES INTO FOUR, and divides again and again in an astonishingly precise and thorough way, producing multiple seeds with three capsules. It is time for us all to do the following:

MAKE A SIMILAR DECISION TO FLOWER,
AND TO PRODUCE SEEDS FOR FUTURE USE,
IN ACCORDANCE WITH OUR OWN DIVINE BLUE-PRINT

Indeed, we are no less than this amazing example of nature's way, nature's abundance and nature's perfection.

The world will become peaceful, beautiful and abundant
IF WE MAINTAIN HOPE IN THE DARKEST OF HOURS

To let go of all hope is to misconceive one's own purpose and capability. It is positioning oneself as a helpless victim, when the very power of knowing that we can make difference, step by small step, can bring us out of that and back into a mode of confidence that the future WILL be bright, DUE TO OUR EFFORT TO MAKE IT SO. If embraced by many people, THIS WILL BE MANIFESTED.

This is the greatest achievement of the dark side - that they have managed to convince us that we are powerless, that our little lives have no meaning, that it is pointless to object, and that hedonism and materialism are really worthy lifestyles which override any sort of altruism or reaching out to others.

Many people are in very difficult situations today,

BECAUSE WE HAVE COLLECTIVELY ALLOWED
OURSELVES TO BECOME ENSLAVED.

Soon, the future may look EVEN DARKER, but the darkest hour comes before the dawn, and if we look with HOPE towards the horizon and march determinedly in that direction, we are bound to experience sunrise.

If we cower and turn away,
the sun will still rise,
but we will not see it.

**The world will become peaceful, beautiful and abundant
IF WE APPLY UNIFYING STRATEGIES
AND ASK FOR SOLUTIONS,
RATHER THAN LETTING RANTS CONTINUE**

These are intense times where many people are polarized into separate positions and opinions. As a result, many rants may occur. As loving or understanding friends or relatives, we may tend to "listen it out", trying to be fair and giving the other person room to vent. However: how long are we going to be this "kind" or "understanding", and what does this attitude bring long-term? It allows the rant to continue, whereas that energy could be re-directed into positive avenues. At some point, we will have to break it off. Or we will just listen meekly, without any chance of expressing our own opinion, or of improving the situation. Or we will violently interrupt because we are fit to bursting point, which means more conflict and more violence.

What are the preferable options here? Unification on all levels, aiming for one common goal, is the ideal. The common goal is a peaceful, beautiful and abundant world for all. To change the direction of a rant, one can ask questions like "But what would you do to change the situation, if everything is possible, so that everyone is happy?" or "How could we get everyone on the same page?" or "How could you use your energy to make a positive change?" These questions may seem simple, but they are EMPOWERING the person who is ranting. They are ranting BECAUSE THEY FEEL POWERLESS TO MAKE A CHANGE IN A SITUATION WHICH THEY PERCEIVE TO BE DREADFUL.

Whatever the situation, we always have a choice whether to listen, whether to ignore, whether to go into conflict, whether to override, or whether to try and further unity towards worthy goals.

**The world will become peaceful, beautiful and abundant
IF WE USE EVERY LARGE AND SMALL OPPORTUNITY
TO INSERT TOKENS OF GRATITUDE AND APPRECIATION
INTO OUR DAY.**

What is the effect if we place a small rose
on the desk of someone we see every day?

Do we not only see but also appreciate that person every day,
either for the love we receive,
or for the lessons we learn through them?

There is always a way in which we can show our appreciation in
small ways. If we are "caught up" in stress, having to get our TO
DO LIST completed within a certain time frame, with no breaks
in-between, there is no time (or we THINK there is no time) to
conduct small acts of courtesy or appreciation.

Is there time to say "I love you?"

It does not take that long. It is only three words, but they are extremely powerful, and they immediately change the atmosphere
- which may be tense or fraught with worry - in a split second.

The even greater step would be to say

"I love you unconditionally".

This would be emulating THE DIVINE, which loves us unconditionally, irrespective of how long we take to learn things, or of
how many deviations we take before finally taking the direction
which is our vocation, our mission, and ultimately, OUR JOY.

There will be those who scream and retort "But how can I love those who curse and abuse? How can I love those who promote corruption and violence?" The way to purge our world of these unfortunate characteristics is to minutely examine ourselves, purging every violent, dishonest and abusive thought from our minds. If everyone did this, the problem would be solved.

If this thought still does not help, then we must ask ourselves if we want to contribute to more violence in the world, by attacking those who are violent, or if we want to create more unconditional love in the world. This does not mean turning a blind eye to criminality; it means finding ways of increasing our love output. For everyone, there will be an opportunity, because DIVINE HAND is placing these opportunities in our way at every juncture, precisely so that we can learn to grow and love more.

The world will become peaceful, beautiful and abundant
IF WE REALISE WE ARE ALL ARTISTS AND IF WE
DEDICATE OUR CREATIVITY TO A WORTHY CAUSE

What is an artist? Someone who examines themselves and their surroundings, discovers what moves them deeply, fuelling their feelings or discoveries into their creative work, whether this is a painting, a sculpture, a design, a dance, a piece of music or a performance. This they do in their OWN UNIQUE STYLE.

If an artist has not yet developed their OWN UNIQUE STYLE, tending to revere and copy others, then they are not telling their own story, but the story of another. They are following, instead of expressing their own views and emotions. They are guided by the whims, styles and fashions of others, rather than paving their own way.

In a way, we are all artists, CREATING OUR OWN LIVES. And indeed, there are "followers" and those who create their own path, whether this is straight and narrow, or whether it contains many stops and detours.

Creativity, therefore, and single-minded purposefulness are two qualities which it is beneficial to promote in ourselves. And when we are all truly and continuously creative beings, developing our own skills for the purpose of uplifting others rather than simply putting our emotions on public display, the world will become beautiful in all its multi-facetted variety.

The world will become peaceful, beautiful and abundant IF WE LEARN TO WAIT

Waiting may be damaging in certain scenarios, such as failing to take action in acute emergencies, yet in other scenarios it has great worth.

You may be inspired to take on a great responsibility or start a huge project, fired up with enthusiasm and determined to make rapid progress immediately at all costs. It is then that you may run into multiple obstacles, or fail to find your way, or struggle to deal with a lot of "red tape" or stumble through areas in which you have no expertise YET. The emphasis here is on the word YET. It is not feasible to acquire, overnight, or even in the short-term, expertise, knowledge and understanding which will take you immediately to your goal. You may well have to stop, WAIT, and look around. You may well have to investigate avenues which have a small but still relevant influence on your course of action. You may have to stop, rest, and "sleep on something" so that you can approach it from a new and wider angle.

It is necessary to have a comprehensive overview of all and to plan meticulously if your project is going to take off. You must also allow for mishaps or sudden changes which influence your project. If you have immersed yourself in all aspects, gathering knowledge as you go, waiting for (instead of forcing) the right time to proceed, releasing ego which urges you to finish earlier rather than later, then everything will run its perfect course.

Perfect does not mean a perfect project: it means that everything happens in a perfect way so that the MOST IS LEARNT. Waiting until one has more knowledge, more facts, more cooperation and a comprehensive overview, so that one can commence with rapidity at the RIGHT TIME, is an essential part of the process.

May you all be creative, flexible and ultimately successful with your various projects in these challenging times.

The world will become peaceful, beautiful and abundant
IF WE NOTICE WHERE WE PLACE OUR FOCUS

Why is it that sometimes we are joyous, dancing around and singing as we complete our chores, while at other times we are deeply despondent, thinking about all the dreadful situations and events happening in our world today?

One day we can be optimistic and open,
and the next we are sorrowful and retiring.

As there are multiple joyous and depressing things occurring at any one time, they cannot be the source of these huge swings in mood. It is not a linear sequence of events - one positive happening followed by a negative happening, and so on - which is causing this and which is reflected in our mood.

We choose where we place our focus. If we choose to place it on things which dissipate quickly, or which provide momentary pleasure, then there will always be an "end" to them. And there is a good chance that we will become addicted to same. If we focus on that which is eternal, without end, such as the love of the earth which provides us with all manner of food and shelter, or the hand of the Divine which is always ready to provide us with spiritual "food and shelter" if we go into meditation and pose our burning questions, then we will never be disappointed of feel any sort of "lack". Thus, we are unaffected by outward circumstances, however negative, because we know without a doubt that we possess the "tools" to deal with it.

The world will become peaceful, beautiful and abundant
IF WE PERIODICALLY WONDER WHETHER THE
OPPOSITE OF OUR BELIEFS IS TRUE

One frequent cause of depression is being fixed upon one line of thought, or fixated on one particular person or issue, to the extent that nothing else matters, in the belief that this is the ultimate truth, paragon or issue of the utmost importance.

To view anything as the pinnacle of perfection is to guarantee "downfall". Those who are aware that life is an eternal flow, where change is the only permanent factor, will be able to "let go" more easily when a larger perspective comes into view.

Others will turn their heads away, clinging to their ideal, and will not be able to adjust to new circumstances or assimilate new information, thus falling into depression.

Those who will fare best in present circumstances are those who can easily say "Oh; it seems I was wrong. Let's have another look at this". May we all include this sentiment into our journey to ease our passage in times where changes are rapid and multiple.

The world will become peaceful, beautiful and abundant
IF WE RESTRAIN FROM USING JARGON

In groups whose members are very familiar with each other and have known each other for a long time and who share the same aims or principles, a feeling of cosiness and of "being family" arises. This happens also to a certain extent in groups brought together by work or other affiliations or organisations.

As a result, a lot of jargon or "in words" or "in jokes" are in use. Irrespective of how welcoming such groups may be to newcomers, "newbies" are suddenly faced with a barrage of new faces, new terms and sentences which they cannot understand.

This is to some extent inevitable, and the newcomers must be patient and learn about what is going on, yet it can be difficult to integrate if the group is led by ego, triumphing over the fact that others are not party to their thoughts and meanings.

This causes division, encouraging EXCLUSIVITY
as opposed to INCLUSIVITY.

There is a saying that all groups move at the pace of the slowest. Anyone who has taken part in a mountain expedition or a self-awareness group, where everyone is trying to move towards a mutual goal, may have encountered this.

If we translate this to a much wider concept - that of the GLOBAL FAMILY - our collective progress is similarly dictated by the slowest learner, IF WE INCLUDE ALL.

It will not help to turn away in smug satisfaction that we have reached our goals, whether it be on a spiritual, mental or material level, if we leave our fellow brothers and sisters on the wayside.

The world will become peaceful, beautiful and abundant
IF WE STOP USING WORDS TO DEFINE THINGS

What is it which prevents us from feeling that we are
all members of a global family, and ultimately,
all created from the same "material" by the same source?

Why are we not united in purpose, walking together in the same
direction towards a worthy goal?

What it that causes division, antagonism, distrust and distress
on levels small and large?

What is the effect of statements like "He is a wealthy, privileged,
high society male" or "I am religious" or "she is a poor, victimized
black woman" or "This is my plot of land" or "Membership is required before you proceed" or "Our rights have never been
heard" or "THAT IS A TREE"?

Perhaps the past statement (THAT IS A TREE) will be the most
surprising to readers. It appears to be a simple statement of fact,
but it is in fact related to all the other questions just mentioned in
that it sets out to DEFINE.

While defining something may be necessary in the course of our
communication, it is also a tool of SEPARATION. The moment
we define one thing, we automatically put ourselves in a position
of being different (in this case, not being a tree, and not being
part of a tree, and not being part of nature to which the tree belongs). This causes a split rather than focussing on the UNITY or
COMMON GROUND which is vital to the well-being of humanity
and the planet.

Here is a wonderful quote from Krishnamurti who stated that
definitions are an "act of violence".

"When you call yourself an Indian or a Muslim or a Christian or a European, or anything else, you are being violent. Do you see why it is violent? Because you are separating yourself from the rest of mankind. When you separate yourself by belief, by nationality, by tradition, it breeds violence. So a man who is seeking to understand violence does not belong to any country, to any religion, to any political party or partial system; he is concerned with the total understanding of mankind."

— Jiddu Krishnamurti

Words are an interim stage. Telepathy - the sending of images and communications via thought - is far superior and reduces such division.

The world will become peaceful, beautiful and abundant IF WE USE ALL FIVE SENSES

During this period in which many are forced into quarantine and lockdown, staying inside has become a new "norm", and thus we are separating ourselves from something which is an essential part of ourselves - nature. And if we feel estranged from this ONE WHOLE, this will result in depression and illness.

It has been scientifically proven that regular walks through forests and meadows have a positive and uplifting effect, not simply on an emotional level but due, for example, to certain chemicals emitted by trees. This is why the essential oils of cedar, cypress or pine have such an uplifting effect if diffused in our rooms and houses.

Walking in nature takes our focus away from computer screens, where we only use our vision and hearing. Touch can also be included, if one is typing, but this is nothing compared to running our hands over the bark of a tree or through the water of a stream. Working with the soil also transfers beneficial energy.

To reduce stress, to relieve the eyes, to allow the development of divine intuition, take a walk through a park or forest if possible, WITHOUT ANY PARTICULAR DESTINATION, following your own impulses, not dictated by anything except your own sense of what attracts you. This allows us to be open for every stone, bush, tree, stream, animal, or birdsong which we encounter. We feel so much more ALIVE than before. I hope that you can all benefit in this way, using every opportunity you may have.

The world will become peaceful, beautiful and abundant
IF WE FOCUS ON MOVEMENT AND CYCLES

Perhaps, in the present times, there have been an increasing number of occasions where we have been struck by a shocking event, making us paralyzed or desperate. We cannot see into the future. We are filled with an overwhelming feeling that this is the end, or that nothing can improve, or that we cannot bear the suffering, either our own suffering, or the suffering of others. We feel that we are up against a brick wall, preventing us from moving on. We feel as if we have been hit by a life-killing blow. We feel that we have lost someone forever.

How do we "keep going" after such setbacks? If this concerns the death of a beloved friend or family, then the shock will be severe and there will be a difficult "period of adjustment" during which we realize what "space" this person filled in our lives. It is our challenge to "breathe into" that space, rather than holding our breath, deeply aware of our own vitality and the vitality of others. This deepens our awareness of loving gestures. It assists us to focus on priorities, including expressing feelings to others.

The whole situation is relieved by the knowledge that

THIS IS NOT A LOSS:
IT IS A TEMPORARY SEPARATION.
NO ONE IS SEPARATE.
WE ARE ALL ONE.
THERE ARE MANY, MANY LIFETIMES.
WE MEET, AND WE PART,
AND WE MEET AGAIN,
AS WAS JUST THE CASE.

We, as souls, are always "on the road". The closer we get, the more likely we are to meet again. To become more aware of life cycles - and breathing cycles on a cosmic scale - is to "let go" on the exhale and regenerate on the inhale.

This can take place on a momentary basis, a life basis, or on a universe basis. There is order, celestial administration and huge cycles in the universe.

So why should there not be order and cycles in our own lives?

If we fall into desperation, we are "holding up" the ending of a cycle and we are preventing our new learning cycle from beginning – a beginning which the universe has organized for us.

Every time there will be "something new and exciting to learn" on our plate.

And so it is today, when a great many people are reaching a level of unprecedented desperation.

This is the end of a cycle - the last dying embers of a great fire - and it is our challenge to continue breathing change.

The world will become peaceful, beautiful and abundant
IF WE LEARN THE ART OF CONVERSATION

Especially in these times of great conflicting opinions (2022), it may be difficult to "get on the same page", yet this is our mandate if we want to become a peaceful and unified world. We must become unified in small portions and groups, which will then automatically lead to global unification in the sense that all are working for one goal, carrying out our duties in harmony.

Many things interfere with the "flow" of a conversation. Conversations may be dragged out needlessly, or they may exclude some participants. The rise of ego - the need to be seen and appreciated - is one of these disturbing factors. Yes, all have a right to be acknowledged, but there is no point in repeating something which has already been said, or which does not contribute in some novel way to the discussion. In such cases, it is better to listen. If we have pertinent information, we are invited to present it succinctly at the right time, without undue elaboration. If we see someone dominating, or wandering off the point, or treating others in a disrespectful way, or automatically shutting down opinions of others with which they disagree, then it is our mandate to make reference to that.

To say the same as our neighbour, or to say something which is already generally known and accepted ("preaching to the choir"), is to promote oneself, waste time and bore our listeners. To insist on speaking although one does not have the necessary expertise (one negative effect of "democracy") is another form of self-importance and lack of appropriate humility.

To cut others off if they are approaching relevant issues is similarly disrespectful. Conversations are balanced exchanges and exploration, not commands or lectures. If we heighten our aware-ness and listen carefully, we can all move forward at a faster pace, and we can raise the level of joy when we meet each other.

"Misunderstandings" which arise during conversation often result from one person insisting on their opinion, while crushing others and refusing to listen. But there is always a bigger picture and more to learn about all situations and conversation partners.

Whereas it is sometimes necessary to stop a conversation be-cause it is descending into violence or has met a "dead end", it will, in the long run, be more beneficial to calm tempers, listen more, and continue talking, leaving a door open.

May all your conversations be fruitful, informative and joyful.

**The world will become peaceful, beautiful and abundant
IF WE RECOGNISE OUR TRUE IDENTITY AND NARRATIVE**

"Searching for oneself", exploring the past, wondering what the future will bring and asking what the meaning of life is are all es-sential parts of the learning journey.

This typically happens when we are younger, when we are de-termining our careers and looking for partners. Many young peo-ple are occupied with searching for stability and direction.

As we move on into our forties, fifties or sixties it is easier to turn around and reflect on what has gone by, and to see which deci-sions led where.

We may also realize that "chance encounters", or opportunities suddenly presented to us, were pivotal events, working in an al-most magical way to further our passage.

However, this is not magical: it is the work of our unseen guides or angels, and they will try to guide us into the direction we NEED (not necessarily what we WANT, on the surface of things) in order to effect true progression, as opposed to temporary highs.

In the course of this searching, those who do not know or remember their parents will be searching for their "identity", perhaps more than others. A stable heritage is a great benefit, yet this is not a firm guarantee of feeling stable in the future. We create our own narrative as we go along, making thousands of decisions every day.

This includes the decisions of what to say when. We develop our personality and - in the best cases - acquire complete self-determination and self-confidence, knowing that all obstacles appear in order to MAKE FASTER PROGRESS, as in preventing us from moving ahead in a dangerous direction.

Thus, our lives are a CO-CREATION. We are given chances, and we are given the free will to decide whether to make use of them or not. It is our task to improve continuously towards perfection.

Perfection is a difficult word for many people, who will reject it outright as an impossible goal, yet this is because they have not yet reached the level of confidence or insight, through their life experiences so far, to realize that

THERE IS NO END TO THE JOURNEY, and that their POTENTIAL IS THEREFORE ENDLESS.

What we are playing out, therefore, is MANIFESTING THE BEST WE CAN.

In other words, MANIFESTING THE DIVINE.

The world will become peaceful, beautiful and abundant
IF WE ARE NEVER LEFT IN THE LURCH

We may be left with the feeling of utter helplessness and desperation, as a result of a sudden shock or someone permanently leaving our lives. Our tendency is to seek revenge, or harbour feelings of being greatly wronged. We feel that developments are unjustified or unfair. We have been "left in the lurch" without any warning, and we grieve that this is so.

How can we see this in another way? If we greatly admire and look up to someone, then we regard them as our saviour, elder or guru, and if we have a problem, we may tend to run to them for advice, solace or "peace of mind". This the guru may be able to give, but the moment he or she suddenly disappears from our lives or from our view, we may fall into deep despair.

However, this is actually the best thing that any guru can do: disappear. As a result, their "believers" or "hangers on" or "disciples" are invited to move from a state of dependence to a state of independence. If we have fully entered our own sovereignty, then we can never be "left in the lurch" because we can RELY ON OURSELVES FOR AN ANSWER. We have not been deserted; WE ARE ASKED NOT TO DESERT OURSELVES.

Another method of counteracting the feeling of being "left in the lurch" is to acquire additional information. If we are critical, inquisitive and searching, then we will gain a fuller picture of what is going on around us. We will therefore be more immune to shocks because we will see problems coming along before they actually "hit", and so we are mentally and physically prepared. If we view things from a wider angle, we are unshockable and unshakable, especially if we are rooted in the knowledge of our own Divinity and our own ability to receive Divine guidance from within.

The knowledge that we are eternal, passing through many incarnations to accumulate knowledge (in the sense of having a spiritual experience), is the great comforter when a person dies or "moves on". They are indeed moving on to the next best experience for them. This should be a reason to rejoice. And another reason to rejoice is that meeting them again is pre-programmed, should both wish it. Thus, one is not "left alone" permanently: one is invited to concentrate on one's own path which will re-join the path of the departed Beloved at a later date.

The world will become peaceful, beautiful and abundant
IF WE REGARD PAST EVENTS WITH HINDSIGHT

Think back to a dreadful thing which happened to you in the past, a number of years ago.

Perhaps you were embarrassed, deceived or abused.
Perhaps you can now see that you had a part in it,
due to lack of discernment, naivety, lack of courage or laziness.

Perhaps, if you think more deeply about where you stand today, you might reflect on this situation and decide that there is a "silver lining" to it all. You may have become stronger or more aware as a result. You may have seen quite clearly that this is a road you do not want to take, and a situation which you do not want to invite again. Knowing what you don't want to experience is a tool towards knowing where you want to go, thus your path into the future is more clearly defined.

The final step of this is to feel grateful for this experience (however horrible the crime), because of the very thorough learning lesson it has given you. The certain knowledge that unpleasant episodes will have some sort of (as yet unseen or unknown) benefit does not solve serious problems, but it makes it easier to bear, when you are in the thick of it. If we reflect with hindsight, we can see the part we have played, and that we are not simply a victim. This empowers us, inspiring us to change our behaviour and to make different decisions which lead to different results.

The world will become peaceful, beautiful and abundant
IF WE DO NOT OVER OR UNDER ESTIMATE OURSELVES

Underestimating ourselves is on a par with cementing ourselves into a limited cage. It means we have already decided that there are certain things we can never achieve. It defies the notion of progress. It prevents us from investing dedication, from following divine intuition, and from mustering the courage to grasp good opportunities. If prevents us from moving on to heights which we never thought possible.

If we look back at our lives with hindsight, and if we imagine remaining in the "prisons" other people would prefer to have kept us, then we can clearly see that we have progressed. Saying "I can't do that" or "that is an impossible dream for me" impose severe limitations and crushes our potential. Our potential, if lived within the framework of cosmic law, is limitless.

Overestimating ourselves occurs if we are so passionate about our dreams and our path, that we forget all else and get things completely out of proportion. To set very high, impossible standards for oneself and for others is programming disappointment and anger all round. Striving for the best, or for a high goal, is very worthy, yet the journey towards it must be carried out in a realistic way, step by step, with regard for others. As in so many other areas, balance is the key.

The world will become peaceful, beautiful and abundant
IF WE CONSCIOUSLY ENTER THE
FIELD OF UNIFIED CONSCIOUSNESS

Some people may immediately ask "What is this field?" It is an unseen but real morphogenetic field which stores and carries all events, thoughts, feelings and memories. It includes everything. We are in it all the time, we contribute to it all the time, and we are affected by it all the time.

The only thing is, we are generally not aware of all this. We are not aware of the fact that if we live in a remote area, for example, living in alignment with nature, and never meeting a single person, the "energy" and "imprint" of our actions will nevertheless enter the earth's genetic mind and remain there to "strengthen" any resolve shown by any other person who is considering the same kind of lifestyle.

Realizing this - the great import of our personal footprint - will simultaneously make us realise our responsibility. Then we will never again say "It will not matter just this once", because everything always matters.

Ideally, everyone would be aware of this, and thus they would VOLUNTARILY CHOOSE to send positive experiences and information into the genetic mind. If this could be achieved, THERE WOULD ONLY BE POSITIVE INFORMATION AND EXPERIENCES TO RETRIEVE. This storage house of positive information and experiences is "tapped into" by earth's populace, as if our minds are downloading information from a computer.

Tapping into DIVINE INFORMATION is similarly possible, because the soul we know as Jesus bestowed us with a copy of his mind (i.e. a library of very positive information and wisdom) when he left this physical realm. This constituted an "upgrade" for everyone, providing us with increased opportunities to improve ourselves and our world.

In the future, if we know we all live and act within this "field of unified consciousness", there will be no need for "traditional" communication. Everyone will be fully telepathic and will be able to feel and sense exactly what is going on. We will be able to correctly assess what the needs and potential of others might be, thus resulting in great understanding, great compassion, and also great creativity and worthy co-creative projects. May our awareness of these possibilities steadily increase.

The world will become peaceful, beautiful and abundant
IF WE STOP GIVING EACH OTHER A GUILTY CONSCIENCE

Imagine a devoted couple who has many responsibilities and activities. Sometimes there is no time at all to relax, not even a moment. Though their lives are fulfilled in one way, managing to complete a wide range of tasks, they are still left frustrated at the end of the day. They are constantly in "giving mode" and they take their responsibilities very seriously. However, they are both on the edge of a breakdown, and they know it.

The man sees that his wife is over-burdened, and tries to arrange "surprises" for her during which he looks after the family and takes over chores. The woman sees that her husband is over-burdened, and tries to arrange "surprises" so that he can recuperate. When these "surprises" are revealed, both are overwhelmed and happy that their partners care for them in this way. Yet they both have guilty consciences because they are getting unexpected "time off", and their concern for their partner - who is taking on even more - increases also.

What is the way out of this situation? Relaxation after work should be routine - an expected occurrence which one has rightfully earned. It is not a rare and unexpected surprise intended to make one feel special, or which is spurred on by the worry of another. Couples need to face this honestly and work it out. It requires discipline, but the profits are untold. To continue with enthusiasm, and to retain one's health and sanity, one needs to know that there will inevitably be a break at a certain time, for a certain length of time. Thus will everyone involved learn to work, rest and evolve.

The world will become peaceful, beautiful and abundant
IF WE NO LONGER TAKE THINGS FOR GRANTED

How many times do we say "thank you" or express gratitude in the course of one day? Counting and recording this is a beneficial tracking method which provides us with new insights. We can also choose to track negative phrases (e.g. oh shit, fuck you, I don't care, it does not matter).

Words have immense power – every one. If we are aware of how much or how little we use a certain phrase, then we can change it, and we can see how the world changes with us, because the world is a reflection of ourselves, and affected by ourselves.

Because we live in this world of our own creation,
we also personally experience
THE EFFECTS OF OUR OWN WORDS AND ACTIONS.

To express gratitude, and to live in a state of constant gratitude, means that we are always seeing things to be grateful for. It is a certain way of seeing and appreciating. If we are in this state of being, this will uplift our spirits. There will be so many things to appreciate, and more and more wonderful experiences will come to us as a result.

If, however, we never look up, keeping our eyes on the ground, deeply involved in depressing thoughts, then we give ourselves no chance to appreciate our surroundings, and thus we remain in that cocoon of self-pity and of non-appreciation.

The world will become peaceful, beautiful and abundant
IF WE CONSTANTLY REVISE AND RE-ASSESS
OUR RELATIONSHIPS

Especially during these periods of "lockdown" when many couples and families are cooped up inside due to "pandemic" protocols, some will be forced to spend much more time with each other in close quarters, without access to the usual modes of distraction or "time out", some of which are forms of escapism and avoidance, and some of which are genuine sources of strength and inspiration. Cut off from these, and from our usual methods of dealing with things, problems may raise their "ugly heads" and refuse to go away before we take a long hard look at them.

In short, this is a huge opportunity to get to know others better - what they love, what inspires them, what they acutely miss, and what is top priority. We may realize that there is so much more that we did not know about them - their lives, their thoughts, their wishes and their needs. And this is also true for oneself. Others may up to this point have been unaware of our own feelings, and these are now forced into the open for others to see, appreciate and take into account.

Could we have really been so wrong about each other? We all have a certain view of our partners or loved ones, and if they do not act according to our expectations, we might say "But this is not the person I know!"

However, it is not possible to really "know" a person in this sense. We are always changing, as others are also changing. It is pointless and irrational to have a fixed image of anyone. Mutual continuous growth is the ideal. Crises will put a stop to usual patterns of behaviour and daily routine. They will shatter the "veneer" and bring out what is lurking underneath. Crises will force us to abruptly reassess, whereas ideally, we should be reassessing all the time. If we constantly reassess, crises will have no effect because we will already be on a deeper level of knowing.

The world will become peaceful, beautiful and abundant
IF WE USE ART AND MUSIC FOR HEALING

THE FIRST TRUE STORY

A man suddenly fell very ill but could not find the cause. A friend who was trying to help him wandered through the house and saw that the man had a new painting hanging above his bed. It was an abstract painting with many wonderful shades of blue. "How long have you had that painting?" asked the friend. "I bought it around the same time that I began to feel ill", replied the man. The friend went up to the painting and looked at it carefully. Barely visible sentences were hidden beneath the layers of blue. These sentences expressed demonic curses, violence, sadness and pain. The ill man was really shocked to discover this, and he removed the painting immediately. From that time on, his illness dissipated rapidly. Such is the power of "negative" art. And by the same logic, such is the benefit of "positive art".

THE SECOND TRUE STORY

A woman was in hospital, suffering from neuralgia - inflammation of a nerve centre in the head. She went into meditation and asked what would help her to heal, and she immediately "received" the thought that some slow, methodical music, such as Mozart's *Masonic Funeral March*, would be effective. She got hold of her mobile phone, searched for the music and then played it, holding it to her head. The pain immediately dissipated. Such is the power of music for healing.

**The world will become peaceful, beautiful and abundant
IF WE ENCOURAGE INDEPENDENCE**

Many people on our world have suffered due to various disadvantages, whether this has financial, social, national, religious, physical or mental causes.

Our first reaction should always be compassion, trying to support them, yet if one continues to be a spokesman for them for their whole lives, they will tend to rely on that support and will never come into their own sovereignty.

This is the dilemma which many people face when trying to help others, which is actually our divine mandate. Knowing how to teach is a great advantage. The best teachers do not simply provide information - they try to draw answers out of us and inspire our curiosity.

Knowing when to stop giving is another dilemma. If we support someone long-term, we are their crutch and we are denying them the chance to grow.

The world will become peaceful, beautiful and abundant
IF WE REALISE THAT OUTER BLOCKAGES CAN BE
REMOVED BY REMOVING INNER BLOCKAGES

This is a basic realization which can relieve extremely acute situations in a very short period of time. Imagine that you are living in a flat and that you do not take out any rubbish for 6 months. Neither do you clean anything, except essentials like the plates you eat off and the coffee cup you drink out of. Imagine that you are also reaching retirement age, and that there are old papers all over the place related to the job you no longer wish to continue. Imagine that your living room is so full of junk that you can hardly find your way to the table. Imagine that your sofa is covered in clothes that need washing. Imagine that you cannot drink a glass of wine, or enjoy a game of chess, because they sit in a cupboard which you cannot get to. In the end, you will not be able to move in any direction. There will be layers of dust everywhere, and everything will start to smell.

Do people enjoy living in this sort of situation? They may seem to be alright, on the surface of things. They may be interesting people with multi-coloured backgrounds and experiences, dedicated to certain causes or capable of inventing things, and they may have critical minds. But in another way, they are also in denial of some very great problem in their lives, which may be a profound lack of self-love. It may also be a form of mental illness, saying that something is clean when it very obviously is not.

The outside reflects the inside; and also, as above, so below. It is necessary to discover the inner obstacles which are hindering the energy flow, so that one can be "in the flow" during usual daily activities. To deny that there is anything wrong, however, will allow the situation to stagnate even further.

The next question is:
IS THERE ANYTHING WRONG WITH OUR WORLD?
And if so, HOW IS IT THE RESULT OF OUR STAGNATION?
There is a lot of "cleaning up" to do, on a mental and a physical level, and we can all contribute to this cleansing process through how we live our personal lives.

The world will become peaceful, beautiful and abundant
IF WE REMOVE FEAR FROM OUR MENTAL LANDSCAPE

It would be very revealing to track a day in our lives, recording all the instances of when fear raises its head. These may be small or large bouts of fear: we may put off telephoning someone who we think has been ignoring us (FEAR OF REJECTION). We may fall into anxiety when we see reports of bombings (FEAR OF DEATH). We may worry about the health of loved ones (FEAR OF PERSONAL LOSS). Insurances profit from high levels of fear, offering all manner of security in the case of our fears manifesting. And the more fearful we are, the more they will manifest.

What would happen if we spent a fear-free day? How would we approach our fellow humans? Spontaneity would be restored, heart-warming encounters would take place, and we would be inspired to carry out many positive actions. Our level of vibration would rise sharply, and we would experience increasing energy. Our sense of joy and wellbeing would radiate out to all we meet. There is another level to this. If something "fearful" occurs, the art is not to be drawn into it, as if this is an incurable tragedy which will haunt us for the rest of our days. It is our task to recognize it as a temporary setback, during which we will learn a great deal, and which is in some way necessary to further our spiritual growth, even if it is only to learn to "let go" and move on, welcoming everything new.

The world will become peaceful beautiful and abundant
IF WE RECOGNISE THAT WE CREATE OUR OWN
HUMDRUMS OF THE FAMILIAR

What is the familiar? Sometimes it is our perception that every day is the same, that our job has sunken into an unchangeable routine, or that our relationship is stale, or that our partners keep making the same "mistakes".

While there is sometimes a real necessity to make changes (a new job, a new partner, a new place to live), stagnation is often due to our own perception. There is nothing like listening to the problems of other people to instigate gratitude in ourselves, transforming our view of our own situation. There is nothing like our partner falling for someone else, even only momentarily, to awaken us to their good qualities, counteracting our conviction that they are becoming more irritating every day.

We may think that we know our jobs, our colleagues, our area of expertise, or our partner. Yet to know something is to place huge limitations. To think that we know someone in their entirety turns them into a creature ruled by routine and habit. It refuses them the opportunity to grow and develop.

It impossible to know anyone inside out.
Their thoughts are their own.
Constant communication is necessary.

If we enquire, and if we persist, we will discover the value of every situation, and of every person, and life will no longer resemble a boring, humdrum existence, but a constantly flowing river of new ideas, situations and encounters.

The world will become peaceful beautiful and abundant
IF WE NEVER LOSE OUR HUMOUR

Here I am not referring to any sort of humour which involves sarcasm, cynicism, self-depreciation or stoic behaviour in unpleasant circumstances.

I refer more to the gentle humour which can gradually tease someone out of their fixed ideas, their conviction that nothing is going right, or their despair that they cannot succeed.

In the course of my journey I have met people who are capable of this, who are in service to "good" and who humbly go about raising people's spirits, reminding them that change is always possible, even in the most difficult situations.

To take oneself "too seriously" is sometimes to separate oneself from others, yet our lives touch others all the time, whether we are in active contact or whether we are living as a hermit in the desert.

The influence of what we do, and the quality of what we are doing, reverberates around the world, affecting others.

If we focus purely upon ourselves, and especially on our own losses, this separation is furthered.

It also encourages others to focus only on themselves, resulting in a disjointed and selfish society.

The world will become peaceful, beautiful and abundant IF WE ASSESS OURSELVES

Assessing ourselves means

CONSTANTLY MONITORING HOW AWARE WE ARE.

An interesting experiment is to track oneself
during the course of one day.

How often in one day do I condemn someone?
How often in one day do I put the blame on someone else?
How often in one day do I give praise?
How often in one day do I express love?

This is not a method which judges.
It simply records HOW OFTEN, not WHAT WAS SAID.

In the end, we might discover that we complained about others
10 times, and that we only gave praise once.

Such discoveries are made by our ability to compare.
We can discern imbalance and correct our behaviour,
without ever a "judgmental" word being said.

The same method can be used in many situations, including
"dieting". Imagine that you can eat anything you want but that
there is a rule in place which orders you to WRITE DOWN
EVERYTHING YOU EAT, down to the last morsel.

At the end of the day you will have gained
a considerable insight into your eating habits,
and you will have a clearer view of what to do about it.

**The world will become peaceful, beautiful and abundant
IF WE ASK QUESTIONS INSTEAD OF
MAKING ASSUMPTIONS**

It is so easy to just lose our temper when we think we are not getting through to someone, when we think that someone refuses to entertain our viewpoint. Often, this is because the focus is on ourselves, in the sense that we think that we are being purposely misunderstood. Yet if the focus is on the other person as opposed to ourselves, and if we consider that this other person is not just being obstinate, and that there is a reason for their stance, the situation might not degenerate into conflict.

There are so many "exterior" factors which may have an influence. The person might be suffering physically, such as long-term pain or lack of sleep, which contributes to irritability. Pain means that one's focus is concentrated on that which is purely essential. Anything else, including prolonged contact with others, is simply too much. This is something we may encounter often with older people whose health is failing, or with those who live under a lot of stress.

But more times than not, irritability is a result of triggering some past issue or unresolved hurt. If, for example, one offers a small criticism and it results in a huge "shit storm", then there is something else going on.

What is that "something else"? If we were aware of it, we would also understand the strong reaction. It is our task to try and understand (without condoning abusive or immoral behaviour) as opposed to "losing it" and condemning the other person as completely unreasonable. Such a reaction is actually unreasonable, but the cause of it is not. If we understand this, we will better be able to remain calm in stormy waters, and we will be better in a position to deepen our relationships, thus making strife obsolete.

**The world will become peaceful, beautiful and abundant
IF WE REALISE THERE IS ALWAYS A DIFFERENT WAY
OF APPROACHING DIFFICULT ISSUES**

There is an exceptionally strong cult of individualism on this planet, deliberately furthered by those who wish to see us divided so that they can tighten the noose of control.

As a result, we often feel that we have to assert ourselves, unforgivingly bulldoze through our agendas with scant regard for others, insisting that our plans and ways are the best. This has been called "self-realization", but in fact it can lead to self-destruction in the long run, self being THE WHOLE GLOBAL SELF as opposed to the individual self.

If we insist on having our own way all the time, we may miss valuable opportunities to gain new insights or to collaborate. If we argue our point until our family and friends can bear it no longer, then we are invited to take a pause from attempting to convince, and to listen to their point of view. They will always have a reason for saying what they do.

To jump into the fray, without knowing the terrain / the opinions / situations / circumstances of others is to fan a fire which would just otherwise just continue simmering.

Great conflagrations are violent. They are sometimes necessary because there is no other way, but they have a very final outcome. Increased "holding back" and "sensitivity" demonstrated by all planetary members will promote peace.

Our listening ability must be up to par with our determination to pull something through, otherwise valuable chances for cooperation, understanding and joy will be swept aside.

The world will become peaceful, beautiful and abundant
IF WE PULL THE PLUG IN TIME

It is up to us to become very wary of what happens around us,
rather than turning a blind eye,
or thinking that it does not really matter.

Everything matters. And if we see a situation stretched to breaking point, we are invited to see why that is, and why we did not
step up earlier to alleviate it, or to turn it around.

If we see something going downhill, in whatever manner, and if
we know that this has the potential for gross disruption or harm,
then it is our responsibility to go into action.

The question remains:

WHAT IS IT THAT STOPS US GOING INTO ACTION?

Often the cause is laziness or fear of the opinions of others if we
"stick out our necks". We may worry or act in a way which may
be perceived to be strict, unfair or "politically incorrect".

Also, some of us may be erroneously convinced that we are not
capable of asserting ourselves against strong odds.

This is a plea to PULL THE PLUG,
however large or small the situation.

It can be as simple as saying to an enthusiastic visitor
I NEED SOME TIME FOR MYSELF NOW.

It can be as earth-shattering as challenging corrupt organizations
of governments. May we all be guided by a moral code which will
benefit others. Failing to do this is the same as inviting tragedy.

The world will become peaceful, beautiful and abundant
IF WE CARRY THE PAST AROUND WITH US
WITHOUT COMMUNICATING

The most difficult problems are those which are not approached, for if they are not tackled head on, they will grow and fester in our memories to exclusion of all else. If we remember that we were insulted or overlooked by someone in the past, some aspect of this will be true, because this is the way we experienced it.

However, are we really aware (especially if we were children at the time) of all factors which contributed to a decision, or all factors which contributed to someone being angry or irritated? Sometimes outbursts from other people have little to do with ourselves, so why should we feel insulted, especially for a long time?

"Digging up the past" may seem like a pointless exercise to many, yet to air past grievances may well help to relieve tense situations and change one's view about what really happened, and why it happened. Without this sort of communication and dialogue, wounds from the past will continue to fester inside us, blocking us in the present.

This is the ultimate benefit of examining the past - to increase present joy and to move unfettered into the future.

To hold on to grievances will depress us.
To forgive and let go allows us to exit the role of victim
and to meet everyone with a joyful heart.

The world will become peaceful, beautiful and abundant
IF WE CLIMB MOUNTAINS SLOWLY

If we focus on our goal alone, desperate to experience the great "success" which reaching that goal will entail, then we are pre-programming our disappointment. We will always be wanting to be in a place which we have not yet "earned", or where our work is not yet up to standard, and in fact if we were suddenly put in that place of success, then we would feel unstable and awkward because these shoes would actually still be too big for us.

Thus, our emphasis should be on the path, on the steps we take one by one with continuous dedication and effort as opposed to massive spurts of energy once in a while. This means that one day, after moving for a long time in one direction, we might suddenly discover that we have already climbed the mountain and that we are now unexpectedly standing on the summit.

This would be true success.
This would be exhilarating.
This would serve as an inspiration to others.

**The world will become peaceful, beautiful and abundant
IF WE INVEST TIME IN OURSELVES**

If we were suddenly stripped of all our "trappings" - our clothes, our belongings, our families and our familiar surroundings - what would be left? This happens when we "die", which is actually going through a door into a new room, only we cannot take anything physical with us.

As young people, we typically accumulate things and build our lives. In the second half of life - if we have gained a certain amount of wisdom - we "let go" and pass our accumulated possessions on to someone we love.

So, what remains in the end? The lessons we have learnt and the skills we have acquired. If we possess skills, we can survive in any situation. If we possess skills, we can create beauty and abundance. And most importantly, if we possess the skills of self-reflection and succeed in mastering ourselves, we can teach this to others and promote peace and understanding.

The world will become peaceful, beautiful and abundant
IF WE DO NOT PANIC

We have probably all felt that horrible feeling of coming to a dead end. We see no way to move forward in our desired direction, or the relationship we cherished is irreparably broken. It seems like we are stuck and helpless in a dark room.

We might scream, cry and panic, thinking this is the end of everything we know, the end of all happiness and of all dreams for the future. We may go into frenzied action in order to try and "save" what we have lost. We may feel we are facing that "dead end" every second of the day. Some of us might even commit suicide in desperation.

We have this feeling because we are facing the wall head on. The solution is not to bang our heads against the wall, and hurt ourselves in the process, but to sit down and wait.

Or we can step back from the wall: from a distance, it may seem less formidable. Or we can look to the right and to the left, which may reveal that there are other paths we never thought of, even if they initially seem less attractive.

Or we can say to ourselves:
"There is a reason for this wall.
It has been placed there by Divine hand,
even if I do not understand why at the moment".

This thought enables us to turn around and look at something completely different. The wall may still be there, but we will be inspired by new vistas and new experiences. And later we will understand why we were "stopped" at that time. And with time, our memory of the wall will not be as an obstacle but as a stepping stone to a better experience.

**The world will become peaceful, beautiful and abundant
IF WE DO NOT SUCCUMB TO PRESSURE**

Young people are often under immense pressure, for example to earn good marks, and to pass examinations. Becoming polite and obedient is another "obligation".

Children are rarely asked to follow their interests: they receive a rigid timetable which does not take any personal preferences into account.

Timetables also chop time into short sections devoted to different subjects, so that it is not possible to delve deeply into something which takes one's interest.

Later on, we may live under the pressure of succumbing to different rules in various jobs, for we are under pressure to earn enough money. We are under pressure from our superiors, unless we opt out of the employment system.

We must also succumb to financial, political, cultural, religious and national stipulations. We are under massive pressure to act in a certain way, use certain words, support certain philosophies and generally to lose all sovereignty.

The opposite of feeling pressure and feeling stressed is to feel free. This is achieved by making our own decisions, thinking independently and following our own path, instead of being governed by tyrants whose intent it is to control us, promote war and generally cause our demise.

To resist, in small and large ways,
is to accelerate the downfall
of such tyrants.

**The world will become peaceful, beautiful and abundant
IF WE DO NOT HELP TOO MUCH**

There are many very compassionate people on the planet, and their lives are orientated towards helping others - all very worthy.

There are two dangers with this, however, if taken to the extreme: the first is, they forget about themselves and their own needs, and so they incapacitate themselves, unable to do what they really want to do (help others).

The second danger is getting pulled into one direction only, such as someone who suddenly demands your exclusive attention.

This is not supporting: this is encouraging a manipulative person to become more manipulative instead of working on themselves and trying to get out of the role of victim.

Ideally, everyone will come into their own sovereignty and take on responsibility for themselves, and for others. This should be conducted in a balanced manner which serves everybody.

It is always beneficial to leave a "gap" in our assistance, so that the person concerned has an opportunity to fill it themselves.

Developing an "imperfect" project allows others to come up with new ideas and contribute.

Thus "perfect" co-creation arises.

ABOUT THE AUTHOR

ART - MUSIC - SERAPHIN MESSAGES - SEMINARS

Rosie Jackson is an author, artist, composer and the founder of *The Spiritual Revolution Project*. This encompasses paintings, music, videos, books and seminars to develop self-awareness. Teaching spiritual principles to promote consciousness, her music and art are powerful catalysts of spiritual uplift. Her *Unity Tarot* illustrates the transformation of 100 global villagers in 2 large paintings and 100 written biographies.

Since 2010, Rosie Jackson has been receiving telepathic messages and visions from the angel, Seraphin. These communications urge us to protect our earth and show us how paradise on earth can be achieved. The messages are presently available in English, German, Italian, Spanish, Dutch and Korean.

Born in England, Rosie Jackson studied German and French and qualified as a teacher. She has worked as an instructor in China, and as a translator, designer and editor for publishing houses and companies in Europe. She now works freelance as an artist, author and spiritual teacher in Germany and Italy.

rosie@rosiejackson.de.

ROSIE JACKSON'S WEBSITES

BUY ART PRINTS:
https://www.artflakes.com/en/s?search=Rosie+Jackson

BUY ART ORIGINALS:
https://www.singulart.com/de/künstler/rosie-jackson-32447

MAIN WEBSITE:
www.rosiejackson.de

MUSIC ALBUM:
https://rjspirit100.bandcamp.com/album/songs-for-the-era-of-light-and-life

SEMINARS:
http://www.rosie-jackson.de/revolution/Seminar_Termine.html

INSTAGRAM:
https://www.instagram.com/rjspirit100/

THE SPIRITUAL REVOLUTION PROJECT:
http://www.rosie-jackson.de/revolution/Projekt_und_Vision.html

MUSIC/ART VIDEOS:
https://www.youtube.com/cha-nel/UCMCeJnqJ9Y7hqAExYmm9iKA

OTHER PUBLICATIONS BY ROSIE JACKSON

The Unity Tarot
ISBN 978-3-754342565

The Complete Seraphin Messages: Volume 1
ISBN 978-3-751976-72-5 (Seraphin Series: Book 4)

The Complete Seraphin Messages: Volume 2
ISBN 978-3-75198150-7 (Seraphin Series: Book 5)

The Complete Seraphin Messages: Volume 3
ISBN 978-3-75190001-0 (Seraphin Series: Book 6)

The Complete Seraphin Messages: Volume 4
ISBN 978-3-752 643275 (Seraphin Series: Book 7)

The Complete Seraphin Messages: Volume 5
ISBN 978-3-753444741 (Seraphin Series: Book 8)

Seraphin's Spirituality School
ISBN 978-3-749485-84-0 (Seraphin Series: Book 1)

The World will become Peaceful, Beautiful and Abundant
ISBN 978-3-751920-66-7 (Seraphin Series: Book 2)

The Peace Parables
ISBN 978-3-750441-51-4 (Seraphin Series: Book 3)

The Absolutely Amazing Activity Book
ISBN 978-3-8370-0238-6

*Wie das Schweinchen Prinzessin Prunella
das Lachen lernte*: ISBN 978-3-749428-85-4

*Ich bin Lebendigkeit: Eine Reise zu mehr Authentizität,
Kraft und Freude*: ISBN 978-3937883-32-8

Rosie Jackson

AN ANGEL SPEAKS
SERAPHIN'S SPIRITUALITY SCHOOL
YOUR DIVINE ROLE:
CREATING AN ERA OF PEACE

ISBN 978-3-749485-84-0. 2019. 292 pages

Seraphin is an angel who send us messages of hope and inspiration, as well as practical advice. Our world requires a drastic makeover, and this will be fueled by a universal change of heart, by widening our perspectives, and by reconnecting to the divine core within us, which impels us to develop our skills in service to humanity.

Seraphin's statements provide remarkable insights, provoke intense reflection, and challenge our limited viewpoint. With great clarity, he points out the necessity for radical change, while knowing that we have the power to implement it. The messages in this book were received telepathically by Rosie Jackson.

This collection of 111 Seraphin Messages has 5 purposes. The first chapter, "Messages from the other side" encouraging readers to start a writing journey, contacting their unseen guides and "downloading" information relevant to their particular task on earth. As your spiritual abilities progress, you will increase in confidence, and you will become a source of inspiration for others.

Secondly, the chapters entitled "Your divine purpose", "Transcending your past", "Creating your future", and "Your relationships", intend to help readers along the spiritual path, assisting them to develop potential, achieve excellency, and use these skills and knowledge for the benefit of all.

Chapter 3, "Preparing for transition", provides advice on how to deal with the intense times ahead. Due to our present position in the photon belt, our planet is showered with highly powered cosmic energies.

These create enormous change, supporting everything of divine nature, and exposing that which is not.

Fourthly, the chapters on rebuilding our world offer instructions on how to address practical problems. They also highlight which qualities we should manifest in order to maintain peace, beauty and abundance on our world.

Fifthly, the goal of the very last chapter, "Reconnecting to the universe", aims to increase our awareness of our galactic neighbours who lovingly observe us. After millennia of "disconnection", we will finally resume our membership of the cosmic family.

Rosie Jackson

THE ABSOLUTELY AMAZING ACTIVITY BOOK OF SNAKES, STARS AND SNOWBALLS
FURTHERING CREATIVE EXPRESSION IN CHILDREN FROM THE AGE OF 7 UP

ISBN: 978-3-8370-0238-6. 80 pages

Each of these 80 pages presents a story, idea, or situation which stimulates children's imagination through questions, suggestions or invitations to wonder what happens next. The pictures they then draw are subconscious images of their inner world, feelings and desires, thus providing their carers with a valuable window to their soul.

Once children are accustomed to expressing their own emotions and needs, they are better able to assess themselves and others on the path towards mutual understanding and peace. Like SNAKES they can shed their old skins, like SNOWBALLS they can move on and grow, reaching more and more towards the stars.

Rosie Jackson

THE UNITY TAROT

CHOOSE A NUMBER BETWEEN 1 AND 100 TO FIND SOLUTIONS

ISBN 978-3-754342565. 241 pages.

100 stories of transformation from around the world

100 qualities which promote harmony and peace

1000 questions which point us in a new, better direction

The Unity Tarot offers a new and novel way of addressing problematic issues. Intuitively choose a number between 1 and 100 and see which positive quality you are invited to increase to solve your dilemma.

The accompanying stories are designed to assist readers on their spiritual journey, opening up new vistas, opportunities and directions. They provide insights, shake up superstitions, encourage action and creativity, dissipate stagnation, break our slave mentality, revive creative powers, invite reassessment and foster true values.

The Unity Tarot has breathtaking potential to implement changes in our outlook, beliefs, behavior and abilities, taking us to the higher level of consciousness which is so necessary for the peace and prosperity of our planet.

THE WORLD WILL BECOME PEACEFUL, BEAUTIFUL AND ABUNDANT

A compact instruction manual:
150 ways to improve our world

ISBN 9783751920667.196 pages

Our desecrated, ravaged earth requires massive overhaul.

WHAT CAN WE DO? This instruction book for individuals and groups presents 150 methods of making the world peaceful, beautiful and abundant. They focus on personal, social, cultural, environmental and global RESPONSIBILITIES. Most important, however, is the recognition of our divine responsibilities:

"We are the drop of water in a polluted ocean. We are a genetically manipulated seed planted in a field which has been doused with artificial fertiliser. We are a small tender plant strangled by rampant weeds. We are a million stars in a far-flung galaxy.

If we can take on these roles, we will ask WHY and search for solutions. If we are in polluted water, we will seek METHODS OF PURIFICATION. If we are a genetically manipulated seed, we will seek METHODS TO REVERSE ADVERSE PROGRAMING. If we are planted in contaminated soil, we will seek METHODS TO REGENERATE NATURALLY. If we are strangled by weeds, we will seek METHODS OF CLEARING THE MENTAL JUNGLE. And if we are a million stars, we will be encouraged to LIVE OUR INFINITE POTENTIAL AND SPREAD LIGHT ETERNALLY".

These poetic as well as practical pearls of wisdom have been provided by the angel Seraphin, and have been received telepathically between 2009 and 2020 by the author and artist, Rosie Jackson.

Rosie Jackson

THE PEACE PARABLES: HOW THE FOOL BECAME GOD, AND OTHER STORIES

ISBN 9783750441514, 140 pages

What do the stories with the titles INSIDE THE MARBLE and THE ROOF and THE EMERGENCY BRAKE have in common? Like the other 53 stories in this volume, they are "peace parables" because they urge us to improve our behaviour, not only for our own benefit, but for the common good, enabling us to co-create a peaceful world. Most of these parables are descriptions of visions received during meditation by the author and artist, Rosie Jackson. Some are adaptations of messages received telepathically from the angel, Seraphin.

One of the most famous storytellers is the soul we call Jesus. Parables are an excellent way of teaching, as they entertain and educate people of various paths simultaneously, without raising an accusing finger. No one is addressed personally. It is up to readers to draw their own conclusions. All these parables are designed to assist readers on their spiritual journey, opening up new vistas, opportunities and directions. The stories provide insights, shake up superstitions, encourage heroic acts, expose corruption, pinpoint our enslaved mentalities, reveal our debilitating dependence, revive our dormant creative powers, invite reassessment of the "status quo", reveal downward spirals, discourage materialism, inspire love of nature and foster true values.

The stories entertain and educate, urging us to search for better solutions, to increase compassion and recognise our interconnection. They illuminate dangerous domino effects, and expose our narrow-mindedness and blind allegiance. These stories prepare us to be flexible in the face of great change, and force us to reflect upon our LIFE'S PURPOSE.

THE SPIRITUAL REVOLUTION PROJECT

In 2005, the artist Rosie Jackson made a mental note of the fact that different people were always sending her the same text which began "If the world was a village of 100 people", and she decided that this was not coincidence, but divine synchronicity. Using the global statistics in this text (concerning nationality, religion, living conditions etc.) she invented 100 "global villagers" – each of whom represented 1% of the global population - and wrote their biographies. Then she depicted these "global villagers" in a 5-metre-long painting entitled THE WORLD-REALITY, illustrating the whole range of human problems on earth.

But having done this, she felt she could not just leave it at that, so she spent another 2 years considering how each of the 100 global villagers could turn their lives around if they pursued a certain "positive" quality (such as respect, gratitude or compassion). Then she painted the 100 figures anew, depicting their transformation, in another large painting entitled THE WORLD-VISION. The 100 positive qualities act as the catalyst for the SPIRITUAL REVOLUTION which can transform our world into paradise. The 100 biographies all have a "happy end" and include 10 pertinent questions, and this now forms the UNITY TAROT which is used as the basis for Rosie's seminars.

100 TRANSFORMATIVE QUALITIES IN THE UNITY TAROT

What qualities must we develop to ensure peace and become "one"? The UNITY TAROT offers 100 "positive" qualities which can serve as a point of orientation. The more we voluntarily and conscientiously adhere to them out of love for ourselves and our fellow humans, the faster we will move towards harmonious living. The transformation of the 100 global villagers does not lie in increased material wealth but in increased demonstration of these positive qualities.

SPIRITUAL REVOLUTION SEMINARS

In the course of these seminars, participants encounter everything which separates them from others (culture, customs, beliefs). At the same time, they discover mutual ground, which is the world of feelings and emotions, how we conduct our relationships, how we deal with our fears and problems, and how we express our sadness and joy.

Simultaneously, participants celebrate their miraculous diversity and potential. As troubadours of a new peaceful age, it is their intent to spread the wisdom, insights and loving attitude acquired during this process. If participants SPECIFICALLY INTEND to represent 1% of the global population, then their personal work on themselves will also positively affect this 1%, working through the morphogenetic field.

The vision of the Spiritual Revolution Project is that these seminars and processes take place worldwide and that participants from many countries built up partnerships with each other. Participants are also invited to search for their chosen "global villager" in real life, and to record their experience in articles / film / photographs as part of the project 100 SEEK 100.

PROJECT: ARTISTS CREATE PEACE

"The arts are not simply for amusement, distraction, representation or financial investment. They are a form of worship or service capable of awakening spiritual faculties and perspectives. We pledge to further the ARTS as A SACRED ACT WHERE EVERY BRUSHSTROKE AND TUNE AND MOVEMENT CAN BE CONDUCTED AS A PRAYER WHICH BLESSES AND ACCELERATES OUR JOURNEY TOWARDS PARADISE"

(From *The Artists' Manifesto*, Rosie Jackson)

FOR YOUR NOTES

FOR YOUR NOTES

FOR YOUR NOTES